MW01593615

What People Are Saying About Bloom Growth OS

"Our hospitality business is on pace for a 22% revenue increase this year ($3.8M growth from $17.2M to $21M), with projections of $33M by 2026 almost doubling in two years.

Bloom Growth didn't just help us set ambitious goals—they gave us the systems, meeting structure, and leadership training to actually achieve them. Unlike other coaching we've tried, Bloom stays engaged throughout the quarter, holding us accountable, keeping us on track, and equipping our leaders to grow. It's been transformative for our business and our team."

—**Robért LeBlanc**, Founder, CEO, and
Creative Director, LeBLANC+SMITH

"As an entrepreneur, I've learned that growth without clarity is chaos. This book brings us back to what truly drives sustainable growth—clarity, alignment, and empowered people. Todd has done a masterful job articulating why a Business Operating System isn't just a framework—it's a lifeline for teams navigating change and scaling with purpose. But the real power goes even deeper: by helping leaders communicate better, own their roles more fully, and trust each other more deeply, it doesn't just grow companies—it enriches the relationships at the heart of them. If you want to scale with purpose instead of stress, and build a business that lasts, this is a must-read."

—**Brian Brault**, Entrepreneur & former Chair
of the Global Board of Directors for the
Entrepreneurs' Organization (EO)

"This is the operating manual for the business you always meant to build. The real value in this book isn't just what it helps you build—it's who you become while building it."

—**Byron McFarland**, Founder and Guide,
The McFarland Group, EO Member

"At year end, it's fast and furious, but with the Bloom Growth OS, we are staying *on track* and *on time*. By all accounts, a wild success. I would not have believed it two months ago."

—**Pam Bellner**, Chief Legal Officer, Copado

"I've witnessed firsthand the transformative power of the Bloom Growth system in driving innovation and success at Copado. By embracing the principles of continuous growth and development, we've been able to stay ahead of the curve in the rapidly evolving Enterprise Application Lifecycle Management landscape. I'm excited to see the Bloom Growth system shared with a wider audience through their upcoming book, and I'm happy to endorse their approach as a key factor in our success."

—**Ted Elliott**, CEO, Copado

"Todd's lessons helped us triple our business in five years, fueled by the growth of our people."

—**Alex Zatvor**, CEO, Destify, YPO & EO Member

"Every business can be improved and every entrepreneur can be helped, which, in turn, brings more value to the world. As a business owner, user, and coach, I have personally been liberated by the Bloom Growth Operating System (BGOS) to live a more connected life with my loved ones.

This transformation comes through raising accountability among our healthy team of leaders and gaining clarity about the future we desire. The system brings simplicity to execution and communication while removing the drama that typically accompanies human teamwork.

Flourish is a practical read that will take you on the Bloom Growth Journey, which is invaluable for creating more time, profit, and personal and professional growth in your life and company. If I could give every entrepreneur a gift, it would be to read this book and apply this system. Your team and family would greatly appreciate it."

—**Gian Marco Palazio**, Serial Entrepreneur, Author, International Coach & Trainer, EO & YPO Member

"Meeting Todd and Isaiah transformed my business. Their teachings—born from real entrepreneurial experience—have challenged me, pushed me into action, and delivered outstanding results. Now, all that wisdom is distilled into a practical, bulletproof growth framework.

Flourish is not a book that caresses you; it confronts you. It doesn't sugarcoat reality—it exposes it. After *Flourish*, the only thing standing between you and the future you want is your courage to take action."

—**Victor Hugo Manzanilla**, Founder of MicroSalt (Now London Stock Exchange Public Company), Bestselling Author & Business Advisor

"In 30 years of leading teams, the Bloom Growth OS is the only system I've seen that delivers both a structured framework for results and the personal development tools to grow the people who grow the business. True organizational transformation requires both the inner work and the outer work—self-aware leaders paired with disciplined execution. This guide distills that formula into a clear, actionable blueprint for success."

—**Patty Campagna**, Founder of Leading Teams,
Executive Coach & EO Forum Trainer

"We are so excited to have these new tools and understanding of how to operate more efficiently as a company! There is no doubt this will help us continue to give great service to our communities and be the best place to work!"

—**Cristina Faucheux**, COO, Moreau Physical Therapy

"Bloom Growth brings humanity to what is often a purely business exercise. It's a framework that drives performance while fostering trust, connection, and a genuine sense of purpose. The result is not just stronger companies, but stronger people."

—**Free Taylor**, YPO Master Coach & Certified Forum Trainer,
Founding Member of the Bloom Growth
Coaching Community

"Bloom reminds us that growth is not a straight line, but a living process—full of seasons, setbacks, and unexpected blossoms. It is an invitation to lean into the work of becoming."

—**Kevin Craig**, Master Coach,
Leadership Catalyst and YPO/EO Forum Trainer

"Todd hits the nail on the head with the four primary growth principles. Making decisive people moves, investing in your culture, growing your team and taking time to celebrate wins is the foundation of every successful growth organization."

—**John Howman**, Vistage Chair & YPO Member,
Milwaukee WI

"When you become an entrepreneur, at some point you pack a bag with a lot of grit, determination and a dream and you head out on an uncharted journey to climb a mountain so you can plant a flag of purpose and freedom at the top. There's no clear and certain path on how to get there and who you will need to become along the way.

This book is THE map that points and leads the way to the personal and professional growth required for any entrepreneur brave enough to commit to the journey. Filled with practical tools and the stories that support them, *Flourish* is an indispensable field guide for every entrepreneur."

—**Aaron Lee**, Founder SIXQ,
EO Global Design Team & Forum Facilitator

"The Bloom Growth system has streamlined our implementation process, making it both easy and efficient. Our coach's leadership in rolling out Bloom Growth meetings and coaching sessions has helped us stay focused, achieve our goals, and execute our growth strategies with greater purpose and efficiency."

—**Al C. Moreau**, III, PT, Moreau Physical Therapy

"Having navigated the complexities of real estate for two decades, I've seen firsthand how easily scaling a business can devolve into chaos without the right systems. Our business coach, Todd Smart, has a truly unique gift for simplifying the complex. His unwavering dedication to the business growth process helped us move beyond mere survival to predictable, sustainable growth.

Todd's no-nonsense, 'cut to the core' approach to team communication and building stronger bonds didn't just transform our operations, it enriched the relationships at the heart of our company. Sustained success is about doing the hard work through an efficient, proven methodology. My advice? If you are committed and obsessed with growing your business, let Todd Smart and his team be your guide."

—**Bryan Pritchard**, Founder/CEO of
Tripcap Investments & YPO Member

Flourish

TRANSFORMING YOUR BUSINESS GROWTH
WITH FOCUS, FREEDOM, AND FUN

Todd Smart
with Isaiah Nolte

FLOURISH

Transforming Your Business Growth with Focus, Freedom, and Fun

For permissions requests, speaking inquiries, and bulk order purchase options, email: hello@bloomgrowth.com.

Bloom Growth
1201 Infinity Court
Lincoln, NE 68512

bloomgrowth.com

Book Architect & Editor: Lori Lynn Enterprises

Cover Design & Interior: Esther Moody

ISBN: 979-8-9999645-0-2

"Love and work are to people what water and sunshine are to plants."

— **Jonathan Haidt**,
The Happiness Hypothesis: Finding
Modern Truth in Ancient Wisdom

Contents

Dedication

For entrepreneurs and team leaders across the globe who are on the field, playing the game full out. For those who love what they do and are willing to fight for the greater good of the business.

You understand the stakes, you want to make a difference, and you're willing to put in the work.

To the entrepreneurs and Bloom Growth Coaches who are doing great work with clients and helped shape the content of this book, including:

Aaron Lee	Gian Marco Palazio	Patty Campagna
Andy Shirk	Jaime Gomez	Ramiro Saborio
Anish Patel	Jeremy Giroir	Ray Chou
Anna Birch	John Glon	Richard Palarea
Brian Brault	Jude Olinger	Rusty Burnside
Cliff Walston	Kevin Craig	Steven Krane
Cohagen Wilkinson	Kim Latko	Steve Thompson
Corey Tisdale	Kim Price	Susan Stevenson
Dan Klein	Matthew Cosgrove	Tim Hoffmeister
Dhiren	Michele Kehrer	Trent Clark
Harchandani	Nick Becker	Wendy Clark
Frank Geßner	Orlando Montañez	

This book is for you.

Foreword

In 2011, the company I founded, Firespring, was floundering. The previous year, our revenue had stalled at $5.4 million, and we were struggling to scale. We had talented people and a vision for impact, but behind the curtain, our operations were messy and reactive.

Like many entrepreneurs, I reached for whatever system or framework I had most recently encountered at a conference or tradeshow. We tried several "flavors of the month," hoping one of them would unlock the next level of growth. None of them did.

Then I met Todd Smart.

Our very first conversation told me something was about to shift. Todd had a way of cutting through the noise, bringing clarity and confidence to the confusion that comes with building a growing business. He offered a framework that was practical, proven, and profoundly human, addressing the real challenges leadership teams face. We hired him to coach our leadership team, and those principles have since evolved into what is now known as Bloom Growth.

The next decade brought results I hadn't imagined possible.

By 2013, just two years into working with Todd, our revenue had soared to $15.1 million. Two years later, in 2015, we hit $30.7 million. But the numbers only tell part of the story. Along the way, Firespring made the Inc. 5000 list five times, became a Certified B Corporation in 2014, and in 2016, was honored by Inc. Magazine as one of the 50 Best Places to Work in America.

Those milestones represented more than business success. They showed us we had finally found our rhythm as a team. We had moved past chaos into clarity, beyond survival mode into genuine flourishing. The principles Todd introduced gave us a path to grow our business while growing as leaders and as people.

Plenty of systems promise efficiency and results. Some work for a while, others disappear as quickly as they arrive. What makes Bloom Growth different is how it addresses a fundamental truth: businesses grow when people do.

Todd and Isaiah have created a system that weaves together execution, communication, and relationships. They understand that clarity of purpose, alignment of vision, and accountability in execution work best when paired with trust, psychological safety, and human flourishing. Without these elements, growth becomes fragile. With them, it becomes both sustainable and energizing.

When I think back to those early days at Firespring, I remember how exhausting everything felt, like we were running hard against a strong current. Todd showed us that with the right framework, growth could feel entirely different. What had been a burden became an adventure. What had drained us began to fuel us.

The shift went beyond our leadership team. Our entire culture began to evolve. People at every level of the organization started showing up differently: more empowered, more connected, more engaged. That's the multiplier effect of a modern growth operating system.

Over the years, I've referred dozens of my peers to Bloom Growth. I've watched entrepreneurs who were ground down by constant firefighting rediscover their passion for their businesses. I've seen leaders get their health back, reconnect with their families, and remember why they started their companies in the first place. I've watched teams move away from silos and suspicion toward clarity and genuine collaboration. The pattern repeats: Bloom Growth reshapes companies by reshaping the people who run them.

This book captures that transformation.

Flourish works as both manual and field guide. It gives you practical tools to scale your business with intention and the deeper wisdom to grow yourself in the process. The book tackles hard truths directly while showing you what becomes possible when you commit to doing the work.

If you're reading this, you're ready for something better. You're ready to stop spinning your wheels and start building momentum with focus, freedom, and genuine enjoyment.

Reading *Flourish* will reshape how you think about your business and how you show up as a leader. It will challenge your assumptions about growth and invite you to lead with both discipline and humanity.

I know this because I've lived it. I've experienced firsthand how Todd, Isaiah, and the Bloom Growth framework turn potential into reality. My hope is that as you work through these pages, you'll discover the same sense of clarity and courage that changed everything for us back in 2011.

When you embrace these principles, growth stops feeling like punishment and starts feeling like possibility.

And when your business flourishes, so do you.

— **Jay Wilkinson**
Founder, Firespring
Founder, Do More Good® Movement

Introduction
A Growth System for Owners and Team Leaders

"The best way to predict the future is to create it."

——————————————————————— Peter Drucker

"Exponential growth looks impossible at first—then inevitable."

——————————————————————— Ray Kurzweil

Pushing the Boulder

"Why are you so afraid to slow down?"

Sitting across from me, staring at the last few bites on his plate, Dan stopped eating. He looked around at the little hole-in-the-wall restaurant, which was our favorite place to meet for a quick lunch.

A fellow business owner and friend, Dan had grown his company from zero to $25 million in less than six years. On the outside looking in, he seemed to have it all—a successful business, a beautiful family, everything he always wanted.

Only one problem. He didn't have the time to enjoy it.

Taking another sip of my sparkling water, I waited for him to answer. Finally, he set down his fork, wiped his hands on his napkin, and looked me in the eye.

"Todd," he said, "I love what I've built. I do. I love it. But ... it's kind of like pushing a boulder up a hill. If you ever take a break, the boulder doesn't stay put. It rolls all the way back down. If I stop now, my entire team and I ... we'll lose everything."

Dan was managing it all—from sales to finance to HR to tech—and the stakes were high. He was in constant emergency mode, but he didn't know what needed to change.

He didn't want to create conflict among his team, so he kept grinding away, working 15-hour days, six days a week. On Sunday, he said he only worked four hours, and he considered that his day off! He had convinced himself that the sacrifice was temporary. He would make up for lost time later.

But you don't get those years back. And you can't buy time.

What many owners don't realize is that by empowering the leadership team (LT), they can all reach the top of that hill together—with increasing energy, predictably, and less effort.

For example, I've seen a business that took 30 years to get to $8 million in annual revenue scale to $22 million within five years of adopting a growth operating system (OS). Others have increased their valuation from $50 million to $200 million by pulling a few simple levers.

What did it take for these companies to double or triple their revenue, exponentially increase their valuation, or prepare for a successful exit—without running themselves and their team into the ground?

That's what you'll learn in the pages to come.

What Is a Growth System?

Not too long ago, growth systems didn't even exist for small to medium sized businesses (SMB). If you were a Fortune 500 company, you had access to growth systems to help you get what you want from your business.

For the entrepreneur, though, those resources were almost nonexistent. They were left to figure it out on their own, taking a piecemeal approach with whatever resources they could find.

The first growth systems originated in the 1950s and have evolved into what I call an execution and communication platform that works through prioritization and simplification.

A growth system isn't some complicated corporate strategy—it's the backbone that turns your good ideas into consistent results. Instead of wondering why some months are great and others are terrible, you get predictable momentum. It's like having the operating instructions for your business, so everyone knows what to do and when to do it, and growth stops feeling like you're pushing a boulder uphill.

Here's what I love about a solid growth system: it makes everything easier and more fun. When your processes actually work, your team stops spinning their wheels and starts moving forward. Your customers notice the difference immediately—things run smoother, problems get solved faster, and they start telling their friends about you. That's when growth becomes easier and momentum builds without leaders having to contribute a Herculean effort each month.

The real magic happens when your growth system gives you the confidence to make bold moves. While your competitors are still figuring things out, you're already adapting and innovating because you have a foundation that works. You're not just reacting to whatever comes your way. You're setting the pace. That's the competitive advantage every business owner dreams of having.

Our approach is not *only* about building a better business by giving teams the tools, structures, priorities, and frameworks they need to gain control and grow but also about human flourishing—building stronger bonds and taking relationships to the next level. You have to grow your people in order to grow your business.

After just a few sessions, we've seen teams transform, shifting from a group of individuals into a cohesive team, moving toward the same goal. Everyone gets clear on their role. They understand the strategy, trust their teammates, and know exactly where they're going.

The change isn't just operational, it's emotional. A spark ignites within them, and they're in sync, following a shared rhythm.

Weekly meetings, once dreaded and unclear, become focused and productive. Tasks that had been benched for months start getting tackled, one after another, with purpose.

Progress gets tracked—and celebrated. The energy shifts. It's like getting an aerial view of an obstacle course, and the team is ready to play to win.

How Did We Get Here?

Businesses that reach the millions milestone often get trapped by their own success, longing for freedom, fun, and forward motion. But what got them here won't get them there.

I know all too well the feeling of building something remarkable only to feel like you're being crushed under the weight of keeping it going.

Over 30 years ago, I grew my first business to over $3 million at the age of 24 and joined Entrepreneurs' Organization (EO) and Vistage (TEC at the time). My peer-group learning was profound, and in 2000, I became an EO Forum Trainer and, in 2003, a Young Presidents' Organization (YPO) Forum Trainer. Training allowed me to do meaningful work with thousands of entrepreneurs, and I started to recognize patterns. In 2011, I began my journey of coaching leadership teams with a Growth OS and have now coached hundreds of teams.

My own transformation journey began with bankruptcy in 1997, a pivotal moment that left me in a confused, disoriented state for a couple of years, questioning what it all meant. This led me to Landmark Education (now Landmark Worldwide), where I experienced my first real exposure to transformation and a completely new way of thinking about myself and relationships.

By 2000, I had become a Forum Trainer, working with entrepreneur peer groups through countless repetitions of growth and breakthrough. Twenty-five years later, you can trace a clear line from that bankruptcy through finding Landmark Education, to becoming a Forum Trainer and Facilitator, and then spending years working with my wife to articulate our personal and family core values.

What emerged from that intensive process was crystal clear: Health and wealth aren't end goals. They're simply tools that allow me to invest time in nurturing and growing my relationships. Because when I really examined what makes life worth living, what gives meaning to all our striving and success, I believe relationships are the foundation of it all. They are what everything else serves.

This recognition culminated in our massive investment in our Relationship Curriculum. Everything I've discovered over the last 30 years, I want that for others, for everybody. We've invested over a million dollars in time and money developing this curriculum because the foundation of it traces back to my bankruptcy and the transformation that followed.

My commitment to family and relationships, paired with the freedom that entrepreneurship provides, led me to take a three-year adventure with my family—RVing across North America for 18 months and sailing the Caribbean for 18 months. This wasn't my typical life. Most of my entrepreneurial journey has been filled with struggle and hard work: working 80-hour weeks, taking three flights a week to three different cities, and living in the constant grind of business travel and long work weeks.

But through my own transformation journey—becoming a Forum Trainer, then a Growth Coach, and implementing a growth system in my own business—I've figured out a better way. My whole journey, going back over 30 years, has led to the businesses and investments I have today, and the opportunity to take this adventure with my family.

I'm living proof that you can have a growing, healthy, thriving organization while having a big adventure. My businesses continue to grow, and it's all possible when you have the right people and processes in place.

The system that became Bloom Growth started as a software tool in 2013 and has evolved into a next-generation Growth OS and an entrepreneurial coaching community. As one of the first 20 Entrepreneurial Operating System (EOS) Implementers® and cofounder of Traction Tools, I gained deep insights into what's working and what's not working in business systems. These insights ultimately gave birth to Bloom Growth.

Through 20+ years of advocacy in forum-based leadership development, I coined the concept of "the 5%" which are the most significant successes and failures that leaders rarely share. This approach has been adopted by both EO and YPO as part of their official curriculum and training materials.

Through my own growth journey, speaking with thousands upon thousands of entrepreneurs, and personally growth-coaching hundreds of leadership teams, I have positively fallen in love with this work. Few things get me as excited as seeing what's possible for business owners and leadership teams—all over the world and across industries.

In addition to business results, leaders who embrace the Bloom Growth Journey consistently report that their top 10 to 20 relationships—both personal and professional—get stronger within the first year.

Clients come to us to spark growth or scale predictably, and we absolutely deliver on that promise. But they also discover they're sleeping better, having real conversations at dinner, and showing up differently in every relationship. The business transformation creates space for everything else to flourish.

A Note to Owners

Most entrepreneurs are incredibly smart people. Many have advanced degrees and have built impressive businesses. But there's a painful irony in entrepreneurship: the very success you've worked so hard to achieve can become the thing that consumes you.

You probably started your business dreaming of control over your time, your decisions, your life. Instead, you've found yourself learning through trial and error, figuring it out as you go, often spending years reinventing the wheel—all while watching your business grow beyond what your people and systems can handle.

Maybe you recognize this scenario: your revenue is climbing, but your systems are breaking. Your team is burned out. You're on blood pressure medication or consume more caffeine than you care to admit. Your friends don't call you anymore because you're always "too busy." The business that was supposed to give you freedom has become a prison where growth feels more like survival.

This is the dark side of business growth that no one talks about. Growth—when done without the right people and processes in place—doesn't just strain a business. It breaks people.

But it doesn't have to be this way. Imagine what could happen if you had access to the same structured, systematic approaches that Fortune 500 companies use to scale sustainably, tailored specifically for growing businesses like yours. That's exactly what Bloom Growth provides.

A Note to Team Leaders

If you're leading a team inside a growing business, you've likely experienced the push and pull of working with a visionary entrepreneur. They bring energy, bold ideas, and an unshakable drive. Their ability to see what's possible is inspiring—but it can also be overwhelming when their vision constantly shifts.

As a team leader, you thrive on clarity, execution, and seeing objectives through to completion. You're after more than just chasing ideas—you want to implement them successfully. But when priorities change on a whim, when a new initiative is introduced before the last one is finished, it can feel like you're constantly shifting gears instead of making real progress.

It's not uncommon for visionary entrepreneurs to return from a conference bursting with fresh ideas, eager to pivot the business in a new direction—without considering how it impacts the team. Meanwhile, you and your colleagues are left scrambling, trying to make sense of a moving target. You want to support innovation, but you also need the stability to do your job well.

This cycle of excitement followed by abrupt change doesn't just slow progress—it creates frustration, stalls momentum, and erodes trust. You're not resistant to change; you just want the space and structure to bring ideas to life in a way that intentionally moves the company forward.

Visionaries don't want to create chaos—they just need help channeling their creativity into action. That's where a strong leadership team comes in. When you have the right people in place, you can help balance big-picture thinking with practical execution. You can guide the business toward real, sustainable growth by ensuring new ideas are vetted, prioritized, and fully executed before the next pivot takes center stage.

Rather than shutting down innovation, this approach gives it the structure it needs to succeed. When the visionary and the team work in harmony—balancing bold ideas with disciplined execution—everyone wins. The business doesn't just grow, it thrives.

Behind the Curtain

One of the most common things I hear from business owners is, "To be honest, I'm afraid to show you how messy things are." Either they've grown so fast they feel like things need to settle down first or they say they need to get their act together because they're not growing fast enough.

But let me ask you ...

Do you clean your house before the housekeeper arrives? Ok, maybe you do. But do you fix your car before taking it to the shop?

Of course not.

And in the same way that cleaning your house or fixing your car before hiring someone to help you would be counterintuitive, so would cleaning up and fixing your business before hiring a Growth Coach.

Adopting a growth operating system doesn't require you to have your business running like a well-oiled machine. Quite the opposite.

An effective Growth OS serves as both the housekeeper (tidying up each room and putting things in order) and the mechanic (fixing things that are foundationally broken and replacing worn out parts).

Many owners and team leaders assume that their business is a mess and that everyone else has it all together. But let me tell you, we've looked under the hood of some enterprise-level businesses, and they're all dealing with the same issues. Believe it or not, "messy" is normal.

When I first started coaching other business owners and team leaders, I was shocked by what I found behind the curtain. (Now, almost nothing surprises me.)

On the outside, many well-known companies seem to be successful and thriving. Their polished, professional image suggests they have it all together. But when I get a closer look at the numbers and people, I often discover that they're quietly struggling.

Without systems in place to create solid structure, even empires will crumble. Every company—big or small—needs a time-tested system that can support sustainable growth.

Countless times, I've heard the owner or leadership team of a rapidly growing business say, "We are really messed up, aren't we?" And I tell them what I tell every client:

"I've yet to meet someone who doesn't feel that their business needs improvement."

Here are just a few examples of situations we've seen:

- One client runs a wildly successful enterprise software company and loves what she does, but she feels trapped. Her business generates millions, but she's on the verge of burnout, desperate to regain control and reclaim her life.
- The owners of a $200 million shrimp processing company want to preserve their company's legacy for their kids, but their differing visions of the future are pulling them in opposing directions.

- A client in his sixties wants to exit his electrical engineering business, but if he were to take his last breath, the business would fall apart without him. Buyers won't touch it because it has no transferable value.

I could give you dozens more examples.

What I've learned is that business owners end up here because they tend to get stuck in the daily cycle of dealing with one crisis after another—with no time to focus on the bigger picture.

Often, it feels as though there's no time to add something else to an already full schedule. If there's no time to improve the business, though, then they're stuck in a never-ending cycle of doing the same things day after day, hoping things will either pick up or slow down. And if you've read *The E-Myth Revisited*, Michael Gerber's classic book on entrepreneurship, you know that ...

The problem is they're working in the business rather than on the business.

Most business frameworks focus exclusively on systems, processes, and metrics. But here's what we've learned after working with thousands of leadership teams: the strongest businesses are built on the strongest relationships. When trust is high, everything else accelerates. When trust is low, even the best strategies fall apart.

That's why the Bloom Growth Journey takes a different path—one that helps both your business and your team flourish together, ultimately creating an organization you genuinely love leading.

— Strategic Growth

"If an egg is broken by an outside force, life ends. If broken by an inside force, life begins. Great things always begin from inside."

——————————————————————— Jim Kwik

"You can have it all. Just not all at once."

——————————————————————— Oprah Winfrey

Hope Is Not a Strategy for Growth

While not growing fast enough is a problem, growing so fast that the wheels are threatening to fall off is just as much of a problem.

When growth outpaces infrastructure, the warning signs are everywhere. Customer complaints spike because fulfillment can't keep pace with sales. Key employees start making costly mistakes because they're stretched too thin. Quality suffers, deadlines slip, and what used to feel exciting starts feeling chaotic. The very momentum that should be propelling you forward becomes the force that threatens to tear everything apart.

Leaders caught in this growth trap often describe the same experience: they're winning by every external measure—revenue up, market share expanding, opportunities multiplying—yet internally, everything feels like it's hanging by a thread. They know they need better systems, stronger processes, and more capable teams, but they're moving too fast to stop and build them. It's like trying to change the tires on a car that's speeding down the highway.

I've worked with countless business owners and team leaders who found themselves in this exact situation. They were crushing their revenue targets, but at the expense of their health, relationships, and sanity.

The stress, the anxiety, the never-ending pressure to keep up—it takes its toll. For every year I've personally spent in a high-growth environment, I probably lost a year of my life to the sheer weight of it all.

The reality is, rapid growth requires resources. Whether you're expanding your team, increasing inventory, upgrading technology, entering new markets, or acquiring competitors, scaling beyond 15% to 30% annually demands significant capital investment.

The challenge is all of these growth strategies require cash upfront, often months before you see returns. Service-based businesses must hire more people. Product-based businesses have to place bigger orders months in advance. The financial strain is relentless.

One of my clients, an entrepreneur in the shoe business, learned this the hard way. His company had nailed its online marketing, and demand was soaring. But they kept running out of their most popular sizes and styles, missing massive sales opportunities.

To keep up, he needed to put another $3 million into inventory—immediately. The problem? That money had to be wired before the products even left the plant, and they wouldn't see a return for at least five months.

Worse, he had no way of knowing if the marketing success they were riding would still be there when the shoes finally arrived.

Despite having a record year in both revenue and profits, his business was suffering. Quality control was slipping. Customer service was overwhelmed. He was growing too fast to manage it all, and the cracks were showing.

Whether a business is growing too fast or they're stuck and not growing fast enough, ironically, they're often both really tight on cash.

One of my clients, Michelle, owns a successful consulting firm. With 80 consultants on her team and a strong demand for their expertise, her firm was experiencing massive growing pains. She knew she needed to hire 40 more consultants in the next year to sustain her company's momentum, but the math wasn't in her favor.

Each new consultant came with a 6-figure salary, meaning Michelle had to come up with over $4 million to bring them on board. The real problem? These new hires wouldn't start generating revenue for at least three months. That meant greater than a million in payroll that she had to float before seeing any return. And even after they became billable, it would take another six months to break even.

Worse, turnover was inevitable. Of the 40 she hired, 10 would likely quit within 18 months, forcing her to start the cycle all over again. If she wanted to keep growing, she would need to hire another 40 the following year—before even recouping her full investment from the first group.

The cash flow strain was nonstop. Every decision felt like a gamble. Hiring too few consultants meant turning down business. Hiring too many could sink her firm. She wasn't just managing people; she was navigating an ever-growing financial puzzle with no room for error.

"Instead of pulling the reins on sales and marketing, why not bolster your other departments so you can ride this growth wave?" I asked her.

"I don't have time. If I slow down even for a moment, the whole thing could fall apart. I just keep hoping everything will work out."

"Michelle," I said, "Hope is not a strategy for growth."

Because she didn't take the time to look at her business objectively and assess which areas needed improvement, she just kept spinning her wheels—until they threatened to fall off.

Without a plan, our nature is to prioritize what's interesting, urgent, or easy. That's like putting your favorite playlist on repeat and expecting to hear something new.

Working together with her team, we crafted a plan to address each risk. As Michelle began to structure her hiring, optimize her training, and fine-tune her sales and marketing strategies, she discovered how to keep cash flow in check while scaling sustainably. Her company is now growing at a rate she can afford.

We've seen that most businesses go through a cash flow analysis based on their business model and find that they can comfortably grow somewhere between 15% and 30% a year, without breaking anything—or anyone—in the process.

This level of growth can often be internally financed. The entrepreneur doesn't have to go take out a huge line of credit or raise outside capital in order to finance this growth. For example, another one of my clients needed a strategic finance leader but didn't think he could afford it. After evaluating existing spending across contractors and employees, his company found that $350,000 was already being spent on their finance function.

With some smart consolidation (shaving $100,000 of current spend), they were able to bring in a fractional CFO for $100,000 to better manage all their financial resources. In the end, they got their needed results at no extra cost. That's strategic thinking and finding a way to win without additional cost.

Many leadership teams haven't had much training in strategic thinking. In some cases, only the owner has ever had the space to be strategic. But being strategic isn't just about having big ideas—it's about prioritizing, simplifying, and focusing.

If you're not growing fast enough, you're often frozen in analysis paralysis while your costs keep climbing. Rent, salaries, insurance, inflation, regulatory costs ... none of these pause while you figure things out. As a result, your top line flatlines while your bottom line bleeds dry.

To escape this trap, you have to make a big, scary bet and make it fast. The longer you wait, the more your margins evaporate. Some leaders can't stomach that level of risk, so they stay stuck while the financial onslaught overtakes them.

Growing between 15% and 30% compounded is awesome. You've got your hands on the levers of how to grow your business, and when your sales and marketing machine is fine-tuned, you get to choose your growth rate.

You Really Can Have It All

You don't have to choose between a successful business and fulfilling relationships. In fact, the most successful leaders have discovered that you can't truly have one without the other.

Harvard's Robert Waldinger reveals in his book *The Good Life* and his viral TED Talk that strong relationships don't just make us happier—they're fundamental to our health and success. As Director of the Harvard Study of Adult Development, now in its second generation and spanning over 85 years, Waldinger oversees the longest-running study on human happiness.

The research shows that while we often think achievements, wealth, or fame will make us happy, the strength of our connections with others actually determines our well-being. Waldinger's conclusion is simple: good relationships keep us happier and healthier, period.

I used to think that I needed to prioritize my health, wealth, and relationships. Now I understand that health and wealth exist to support human connection. That's why I'm so passionate about building winning teams and fostering deep bonds, creating transformation that extends far beyond the workplace.

One Bloom Growth Operating System (BGOS) client, a Latin American company in the tech space specializing in staff augmentation, was at a turning point when they began working with Isaiah, my coauthor and fellow Growth Coach. They were generating $4.1 million in revenue with razor-thin profit margins of 4%. The leadership team was fractured, and planning sessions left them frustrated and drained.

During their first full off-site (Bloom Day 1), the owner and operations leader called it "a breath of fresh air." In the past, these sessions would drag on until late at night, often ending with tempers flaring.

The initial steps were tough. They needed to overhaul their leadership team, a process that took over a year. As Jim Collins puts it, "The people who got you here may not be the ones to get you there."

The results were impressive. In just the first year, their revenue grew by 26%, from $4.1 million to $5.2 million. The following year, they achieved 34% growth and hit record profits, with margins climbing from 4% to 19%.

But the most profound impact wasn't on their bottom line—it was on their overall quality of life.

Before they started their Bloom Growth Journey, the owner was deeply entrenched in the weeds, running every department, answering endless questions, and solving problems that others could have handled. It was a constant cycle of frustration and exhaustion.

Over the past few quarters, everything changed. With clear systems and empowered department leaders, the owner stepped back from day-to-day operations and embraced his role as visionary.

For the first time, he was free to focus on high-value activities like building relationships and cultivating business opportunities. He even started taking top clients—brands like Pepsi and Under Armour—on motorcycle trips, riding through beaches and mountains, creating unforgettable experiences that strengthened bonds and generated new business.

Focusing on his unique strengths and passions freed up more time. By moving from the weeds to the lead, he unlocked more value for the business while rediscovering the joy of entrepreneurship.

Focused Execution

Before embarking on the Bloom Growth Journey, Isaiah's client was stuck in what Stephen Covey calls "the thick of thin things"—busy but not productive, pushing through daily tasks while the big, crucial goals that would truly move the company forward kept slipping through the cracks. The new system gave them the structure and focus they were missing, allowing them to work smarter, not harder.

With Bloom Growth OS and its intuitive software, they now know exactly what to focus on. As Peter Drucker famously said, "What gets measured gets managed," and the system's goal tracking lets teams see exactly where they stand, what's on the horizon, and what needs their attention.

But the transformation goes deeper than productivity. Leaders get to enjoy the journey again—they have space to spend time with their families, nurture their passions, and create meaningful experiences for themselves, their teams, and the people their businesses touch.

The journey begins with a candid assessment of where you're at and creating a 5-Year Vision. Without a clear destination, progress is meaningless—you could be moving away from your ideal future. You don't get in the car and start driving without first deciding where you are going, yet people do it in business all the time.

With a well-defined vision, every decision, every adjustment, and every achievement aligns toward a future where the company thrives, teams stay engaged, and success becomes predictable. This clarity transforms how leaders operate—they stop reacting to whatever feels urgent and start responding to what actually moves them forward.

When you're no longer just busy but moving with purpose, making real progress toward your goals with renewed clarity and energy, the transformation is remarkable. To witness and be part of that level of change is both deeply rewarding and absolutely thrilling.

The Four Primary Growth Principles

All of our high-growth clients—those growing 20% to 100% annually—intentionally focus on the following four primary growth principles:

1. **Decisive People Moves**: Too many organizations hit a constraint here. My advice? Make the decision. If you need support, consult HR or legal, but act. Delaying people decisions hurts twice—once in business results, and again in the stress and guilt leaders carry from avoiding what they know needs to be done.
2. **Obsess and Invest in Culture**: The most successful teams are the ones who are connecting relationally and having the most fun. Growth doesn't lead to fun. Connection leads to fun, which leads to sustainable growth.
3. **Growing Your People**: Be known as a destination employer. For example, one of my clients, a top-tier landscape architecture firm, has a reputation as the best place for graduates to launch their careers. That reputation draws the best talent and strengthens their business. Become the best

training organization in your entire industry and watch business results come along for the ride.

4. **Celebrating Success:** Wins can get overshadowed and forgotten or, worse, discouraged. Too many companies have what I call a "sales prevention department." The sales team brings in a large client or a new opportunity, and the operations team responds with, "How in the world are we going to handle this?" Suddenly, the sales leader feels the need to apologize for the sale instead of celebrating it. Successes, no matter how small, should be recognized and celebrated with abundance and gratitude.

These principles work together as a reinforcing system. When you make decisive people moves, you create space for better culture. When you invest in training and developing your people, they naturally want to celebrate wins together. And when you celebrate growth, you attract the kind of people who thrive in that environment. High-growth companies don't just implement these principles—they make them habits that compound over time.

Farther, Faster, with Fewer Struggles

The most successful leaders don't make it to the top alone. They surround themselves with people who know how to get there.

As the saying goes, "If you want to go fast, go alone. If you want to go far, go together." But if you want to go farther faster, with fewer struggles, go together—with a coach.

Bringing in a Growth Coach to create better team alignment, clarity of focus, and a culture of servant leadership may be the change that's needed to break the cycle. They help identify processes to optimize, obstacles to remove, and opportunities to leverage.

If you're looking for measurable returns, whether it's through a combination of increased revenue, higher efficiency, or a stronger leadership team working together with clear direction from an experienced coach, you may be ready for Bloom Growth OS.

You might be thinking, "This sounds exactly like what we need, but I'm not sure where to start." Chances are, you're not reading this book because everything's running smoothly. You're probably here because you want something different—more predictable growth, better team dynamics, or maybe just the freedom to step away without everything falling apart.

If you're curious about what that could look like for your business specifically, I'd encourage you to book a call with the Bloom Growth Coach who gave you this book or another one of our experienced Bloom Growth Coaches. They'll spend 30 minutes understanding what's really happening in your business right now—the challenges that keep you up at night, the goals that feel just out of reach. Together, you can map out a clear path forward that actually fits your unique situation.

To have a real-world entrepreneur who has successfully faced similar challenges speak to your leadership team about your company's untapped potential, scan the QR code below or reach out to the Bloom Growth Coach who shared this book with you.

Get Connected

Jeremy Giroir
Bloom Growth Coach

+1 337.298.8323

bloomgrowthcoach.com/get-connected

——Winning Teams

"If you think the price of winning is too high, wait till you get the bill from regret—and that bill from regret is generational."

——— Tim Grover

"Leadership is not about being in charge. It is about taking care of those in your charge."

——— Simon Sinek

Building a Winning Team

Business owners and executive leadership teams get a finite number of chances to create something truly impactful and deeply fulfilling.

Think about it: most professionals have roughly 40 good working years, giving them only three or four meaningful shots at building or being part of an exceptional team that makes a dent in the world while making work genuinely enjoyable.

On average, the journey from starting a business to a successful exit spans 15+ years, yet the public typically sees only the final four—the culmination of years of grit, growth, and determination.

When was the last time you felt you were part of a winning team? When I ask leaders this question, the responses are telling. Only about 20% of people recall experiencing this in a workplace setting. For most, the memory goes all the way back to sports teams in high school.

That's heartbreaking to me—especially since feeling the thrill of being on a winning team is so fulfilling. Our most successful clients tell us that the key to building a thriving business started with building an exceptional team.

For example, I had a client who sold their company for $215 million. When we began working together, the business was valued at around $45 million.

I asked the leader what made the biggest difference in 4X-ing the company's value during our time together.

Now, this was a company with a 75-year legacy. And yet, they were able to quadruple their value within a five-year window.

He paused for a good 60 seconds, really thinking it through. And then he said: "It was getting the right people in the right seats on the leadership team."

Once they had a winning leadership team in place, those leaders went on to build out their departments to be just as strong.

The Magic of "Right People, Right Seats"

While getting the right people in the right seats with decisive people moves tends to be the first critical step toward massive growth, it's the one that often gets avoided.

Why?

In the beginning, when the business is gaining momentum, you're hiring generalists who can adjust to the constantly changing environment, but when your business reaches a certain level of revenue, you'll want to seek out specialists for each department.

Although successful businesses are often described as well-oiled machines, they're more like living organisms— greater than the sum of their parts and driven by the synergy of everyone involved.

When my kids were little, we watched a movie called *Eight Below*, which is about a sled dog team. If you've ever seen a champion sled team in motion, it's a thing of beauty—fast, coordinated, powerful.

Behind that seamless performance is careful planning and precise positioning. Each one has a specific role, and if they're not in the right place or working in perfect sync, the sled won't move, no matter how talented the individual animals might be.

Lead dogs set the pace and make quick decisions. They may not be the strongest, but they're smart, focused, and trusted. Think of them as your strategists and big-picture thinkers.

Next come the swing dogs. They guide the team through turns and translate vision into action—your managers and department heads.

Then, the team dogs: the steady force keeping things moving. They're not often in the spotlight, but they're essential. Think HR and finance.

At the back are the wheel dogs, the muscle. They pull the sled's weight, especially on tough terrain. That's ops, sales, and marketing—always creating and sustaining forward progress.

Now imagine what would happen if you were to mix up these roles. A strong but hesitant lead dog can't effectively guide the team. If the middle doesn't pull together, progress stalls.

The best teams, like the best sled dog packs, run on trust, clear roles, and communication. And like a good musher, a great visionary knows when to push and when to let the team rest, maintaining pace without burnout.

This is the power of getting your right people in their right seats. Just like that sled team, when everyone understands their role and trusts the people around them, they can achieve something far greater than the sum of their individual efforts.

When you have steady, clear communication flowing and the team is aligned toward an ideal future, it's positively magical.

Exceptional teams don't come together by chance. They're the result of focused intention, consistent execution, and a relentless commitment to pushing beyond what they thought possible.

As a leader, your job is to foster a culture where this mindset thrives. When the team is aligned, the goals are clear, and the results are celebrated, that's when winning becomes a way of life. It isn't an annual event; it's a daily practice.

What we've discovered through coaching thousands of leadership teams—and what our software has validated across more than 500,000 leaders and 14,000 companies— is that there are 8 Essentials that all successful businesses have in place.

Many high-performing teams think they need to change 50 things or focus on 25 areas to move the needle in their business. In reality, most businesses typically only need to focus on two or three of the 8 Essentials to begin seeing significant changes in their growth trajectory.

These 8 Essentials are practical, proven pillars that help unlock the hidden potential in your organization.

attracts and retains top talent. Annual Goals focus on must-win priorities, while Quarterly Priorities break e into 90-day sprints.

out this clarity, teams drift. With it, they move with ose, making every decision simpler because everyone ws exactly where you're headed.

eople

you have a clear org chart? Are the right people in the t seats? Defining roles and responsibilities is key to ing sure everyone knows where they fit and how they tribute.

focus here is on setting expectations, identifying gaps, laying the groundwork for management training. That udes teaching interviewing skills, creating a culture of ctive feedback, and building systems for reviews, rais- and meaningful incentives.

h growth comes more sophisticated styles centered on vant-leadership—where leaders prioritize the growth d well-being of their team members and themselves. her than holding your direct reports accountable, i're humbly helping your direct reports win.

Meetings

etings shouldn't feel like a waste of time—and they n't when built with intention. We help teams design a curring meeting rhythm that drives alignment, account- ility, and action across the organization.

e system includes clear agendas and consistent cadences: eekly leadership team meetings, all-company updates,

The next five years won't happen by accic   that
shaped by the foundation you build startir   5-7
we explore these 8 Essentials, we'll explor   the
overview of the Bloom Growth Journey—f
90 days through year upon year of sustaine   Wit
                                                   pur
Let's take a quick tour through each one.   knc

The Bloom 8 Essentials

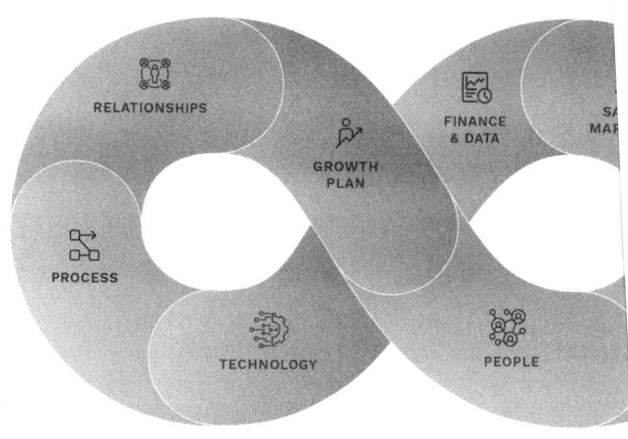

1. Growth Plan

Growth starts with clarity. A solid Growth P
alignment around where you're going, why it n
what it will take to get there. This one-page bl
cludes your What (the raw, authentic descripti
you do), How (your unique approach in 3-7 w
Why (your heartfelt purpose beyond profit).

Your 5-Year Vision serves as the north star—b
ingful and measurable. The 3-Year Future paint:

2.

Do
rig
ma
co

Th
an
inc
eff
es,

W
se
an
Ra
yc

3.

M
d
re
a

T
v

quarterly planning sessions, departmental check-ins, monthly financial reviews, growth-oriented 1:1 meetings.

With fewer total meeting minutes following a next-level structure, you'll unlock faster decisions, stronger communication, and infinitely better results. Effective meetings are a powerful growth accelerator.

4. Sales & Marketing

Revenue growth comes from two engines: acquiring new clients and expanding existing relationships. It's hard to optimize what you can't see, so we start by mapping the entire client journey. This gives teams clarity on how prospects become clients, and how clients turn into loyal advocates who generate referrals.

With that foundation in place, we build out a go-to-market (GTM) and sales process that aligns with the company's ideal client profile (ICP). Your pricing strategy, positioning, and promotional approach all get aligned around what your audience actually needs—and what your team can consistently deliver.

When your sales and marketing efforts are targeted, consistent, and connected to your ideal clients, growth becomes predictable. Equally important is retaining and growing existing clients—often your most profitable revenue source. The best teams don't just focus on new business; they systematically nurture current relationships for expansion opportunities and referrals.

5. Finance & Data

You can't manage what you don't measure. Financial clarity requires knowing your numbers—revenue, margins, cash flow, and key performance indicators (KPIs)—to make smart, timely decisions. Start with a solid financial plan: clear budgeting, priority-aligned spending, and visibility into performance drivers. By Q1 of Year 2, we focus on profit optimization—increasing margins and maximizing return on effort. Understanding your numbers replaces leadership anxiety with confidence, allowing you to guide your business with vision rather than fear.

6. Technology

Tech should simplify your business, not complicate it. The right technology stack is crucial for organizational growth, supporting communication, documentation, project management, and performance tracking.

The biggest challenge isn't learning to use technology but finding the time to properly vet what you actually need. Teams often discover their current tech isn't being fully used, leading them to add new software even though their existing platforms already have the required features. This creates redundant spending and fragmented workflows because there's no time to thoroughly explore existing tools, so teams default to adding another platform for each specific function.

By evaluating what works, what doesn't, and what's missing while ensuring your entire organization is aligned and trained on your tech, you can build a tech ecosystem that saves time, reduces friction, and empowers your team to execute with confidence.

Including Bloom's software in your tech stack helps increase the effectiveness of your meetings and track your entire growth journey in a streamlined, automated way.

When evaluating your tech, you'll want to optimize internally as well as leverage externally. Optimizing internally means auditing your tech stack to eliminate overlapping subscriptions (teams often discover 10–20% waste from duplicate software across departments). Leveraging externally means using technology strategically with prospects and customers, making their experience seamless while positioning your company as innovative and professional. This dual approach reduces costs internally while increasing close rates and referrals externally.

7. Process

Goals are for people who want to win once—processes are for people who want to win over and over and over. Process is all about improving the speed and quality of all the recurring tasks, reducing rework, creating repeatable workflows, and documenting them in a way your team actually uses them.

Whether it's marketing, sales, ops, finance, or training, the goal is a system that evolves with your business. When your systems are clear, current, and centralized, your team moves faster, makes fewer mistakes, and scaling becomes a whole lot smoother.

8. Relationships

Putting a focus on relationships develops emotionally intelligent leaders who recognize that true organizational change starts with inner work, building on a foundation of psychological safety, challenging limiting beliefs, and fostering emotional connection. Leaders move from simply reacting to consciously responding and shift from managing their own challenges to designing environments where everyone can thrive.

At Bloom, our Relationship Curriculum is structured around five core capabilities: Self-Awareness, Emotional Mastery, Relational Skills, Influence and Impact, and Human Flourishing. By mastering these, leaders transform not only their personal and professional relationships, but also their ability to inspire and lead with purpose.

Ultimately, the Relationship Curriculum cultivates leaders who become architects of human potential. They do more than deliver results—they elevate everyone around them, creating a lasting legacy of abundance, connection, and mutual support.

Making the Complex Simple

If these 8 Essentials feel overwhelming at first glance, take a breath. That's exactly why Bloom Growth exists. Through working with over 14,000 teams across multiple industries and 56 countries, we specialize in making the complex simple. You're not tackling this alone, or all at once.

The beauty of these essentials is their simplicity when properly prioritized. Most businesses see dramatic shifts by focusing on just two or three areas where they have the biggest gaps. Your Bloom Growth Coach will help you identify exactly where to start and guide you step-by-step through the process.

Here's what we see time and again: companies that look polished from the outside are often held together internally by makeshift solutions and patched-together processes. We've worked with businesses with revenues of $5 million or even $200 million annually that are still running on duct tape foundations. The Bloom Growth Journey starts by addressing this hidden chaos, transforming it into clear, manageable systems.

The magic lies in our proven approach and entrepreneurial coaches who've seen every scenario. What initially looks like eight overwhelming areas becomes a clear, manageable path forward. As these fundamentals fall into place, you'll find that running your business becomes energizing rather than exhausting and the work you do aligns with the life you want to live.

Your Roadmap to Sustained Success

The Bloom Growth Operating System is a structured, coach-guided journey spanning multiple years. It begins with foundational, full-day, offsite strategic planning sessions at specific intervals (Bloom Days 1, 30, 60, and 90), including check-ins between these days. Following this 90-day foundation, the journey continues with quarterly planning sessions and annual strategic reviews throughout Years 1, 2, 3, and beyond, all guided by a certified Bloom Growth Coach.

This isn't a one-time workshop or a book you read and put on the shelf. It's an ongoing partnership with your coach and leadership team, where each planning session builds on the previous one to establish momentum and allow for necessary adjustments.

Your Bloom Growth Coach will guide you through implementing the 8 Essentials, help you navigate challenges, celebrate wins, and ensure that the growth you achieve is both sustainable and scalable. The structured timeline creates guardrails and rhythm, while the coaching relationship provides the expertise and outside perspective that every leadership team needs to reach their full potential.

An Interview with Steven Krane— Over 40 Years in the Wrong Seat

Steven Krane is a serial entrepreneur and successful Bloom Growth Coach who has helped transform dozens of multi-million dollar companies.

I started my first business at 17, and during my next four decades as an entrepreneur, I often thought, "I wish I had an MBA, or I wish I had spent a few years in a Fortune 500 company to learn how they operate." I was completely self-taught, learning as I went, figuring things out through trial and error.

I spent years reinventing the wheel, learning lessons the hard way, missing opportunities for growth simply because I didn't know what I didn't know.

For most of my career, I served as both the visionary and the operator in my businesses. I brought the ideas, raised the funds, assembled the teams, but I also tried to handle the day-to-day operations. I thought that's what successful entrepreneurs did.

The breakthrough came only recently when, during a coaching session, I realized I was always in the wrong role. I'm not the operator. I'm the visionary. By forcing myself into the wrong seat, I was holding myself and my companies back for decades.

Understanding this has been transformative, not just for the companies I coach but for my own professional growth.

Now, when I walk into a $30 million company and see a visionary leader causing havoc with their constant pivoting, I'm not afraid to call them out. I'll look them in the eye and say, "You're causing chaos. You need to step back and let the team execute."

I can say this because I recognize the patterns from my own experience.

These conversations are rarely easy, but they're always necessary. What I've found is that once the visionary understands the impact of their behavior, they're often relieved. They don't want to be the source of chaos. They simply need someone to guide them toward a better way of leading.

I remember one CEO who was constantly introducing new initiatives. His team was exhausted, spinning their wheels on half-finished projects. When I approached him about it, he initially pushed back. But within weeks, once he stepped back and let his team focus, the transformation was remarkable.

The excitement among his team became palpable. They adopted a weekly meeting cadence that kept them focused. Long-neglected to-do lists, some gathering dust for years, were tackled systematically. They weren't just talking about goals anymore. They were achieving them.

That's when I knew I'd found my calling.

Helping these businesses transform has given me a deep sense of satisfaction. More than I've ever felt in my 43 years of starting and running companies.

I've always been passionate about connecting people and helping businesses succeed. But through this work, I've gone beyond networking and advice, diving deep into the core of companies to help them rebuild from the inside out. When you've lived the chaos yourself, you know exactly how to help others find their way out of it.

Steven Krane,
Serial Entrepreneur & Bloom Growth Coach

───Relationships
Everyone Becoming the Best Version of Themselves

"Until you make the unconscious conscious,
it will direct your life and you will call it fate."
─────────────────────────────── Carl Jung

"Work is love made visible."
─────────────────────────────── Kahlil Gibran

The Groundwork for Transformation

The most powerful business transformations we've witnessed all have something in common: they begin when leadership teams get honest about how they're actually working together—and commit to elevating that experience.

By addressing the relationship dynamics that drive every decision, every conflict resolution, and every pivotal situation, we create a foundation for sustainable growth.

Most leadership programs focus on team dynamics and communication frameworks, which are valuable tools. However, the most powerful breakthroughs happen when leaders do the deeper work to understand their own patterns and triggers. This awareness helps them recognize and navigate relationship traps before these patterns slow down decisions or create unnecessary friction.

This isn't a weekend workshop or quarterly team-building exercise. It's a comprehensive, two-and-a-half to three-year journey that transforms how leaders understand themselves, relate to each other and, ultimately, how the entire company performs in the marketplace.

What makes this approach revolutionary isn't just the comprehensiveness of the curriculum—it's the recognition that to develop leaders, we must address the whole person.

Technical skills without inner work create leaders who can execute but can't inspire. Inner work without practical application creates self-aware leaders who can't drive results.

Aligned leadership teams who communicate with emotional intelligence don't just implement strategies—they bring them to life with energy and focus.

Developing Leaders Who Elevate Others

The ultimate vision for our Relationship Curriculum is to develop leaders who unlock the potential in everyone around them. This means going beyond just completing tasks and hitting goals to actually helping people grow, feel connected to their work and teammates, and find joy and fulfillment in what they do every day. We focus on creating lasting positive change that makes work feel meaningful and energizing for everyone involved.

Our Relationship Curriculum focuses on five key areas:

1. **Self-Awareness**
2. **Emotional Mastery**
3. **Relational Skills**
4. **Influence and Impact**
5. **Human Flourishing**

The first four build sequentially on each other, moving from inner work to outer impact, while the fifth—human flourishing—acts as a transformative superpower that amplifies everything else.

When leaders develop these abilities, they transform their personal and work relationships while becoming more skilled at motivating others and leading with clear purpose.

Leaders explore their organization's purpose and align it with their own personal purpose—but this alignment is only possible when they've first gotten clear about who they are at their core.

The first step is to establish an environment where leaders feel safe to share their beliefs, stories, and leadership styles without fear of judgment or attack. But this external safety can only be created when leaders have done the internal work to feel safe with themselves first.

When leaders feel psychologically safe—both internally and externally—they're willing to examine their deepest assumptions and most vulnerable areas of growth.

The first 90 days of coaching serve three critical functions that make everything else possible:

- Creating psychological safety and trust
- Challenging beliefs and assumptions
- Building emotional connection and deeper bonds

Without these in place, the depth and quality of conversation required for Years 1 and 2 cannot happen.

The Danger in the Stories We Tell Ourselves

Once trust is established, we focus on challenging the limiting beliefs and stories we tell ourselves. This involves becoming self-aware of the assumptions we hold that are actually leading to suboptimal outcomes.

During Day 30, we introduce a conversation about unconscious limiting beliefs or negative narratives we've created. When teams get stuck in these—whether about themselves, their teammates, their direct reports, or leadership—it slows everything down. It creates drama, drains energy, and disrupts execution.

When people have that *aha* moment and start practicing self-awareness around these patterns, the team's performance improves.

Isaiah shares a story about a teammate who spent a week worried he'd be fired, simply because his boss asked him to document a conversation and email it to him. That single assumption messed with his head—and his performance—until they talked and cleared it up.

This kind of thing happens all the time. When people stop creating limiting narratives, they free up so much energy to actually do their jobs.

Taking the time to identify the assumptions we're making and evaluate their validity helps to break the cycle of overthinking.

Everyone does it to some extent—we take something that happened, create a meaning around it, and then treat that meaning as reality. That's how people end up stuck in mental loops, wasting energy.

Some people get so caught up in it that they stop functioning effectively. It's one of the reasons therapy exists—to help unwind these thought patterns.

This work is deeply inspiring, but it's also confronting. It raises awareness—not just about leadership, but also about what it means to be human.

From Reacting to Responding

Within the first year of the Bloom Growth Journey, we have a conversation about trigger management and what we call "robustness."

Trigger Management involves consciously mapping what causes your biggest emotional reactions, understanding the biological processes at work, and designing intentional responses that are aligned with your values.

Robustness goes beyond resilience. While resilience is about bouncing back after being knocked down, robustness is about having proactive systems that allow you to sail through adversity with composure and presence. You are already likely a great firefighter; this is about becoming great at fire prevention.

Many leaders live in a world of reaction—something happens, they react automatically, then spend considerable time recovering from reactions they wish they hadn't made. When you're reacting, you're not leading.

Let's say, for example, that you've worked all week on an important presentation. You've double-checked the numbers, refined your slides, and even rehearsed in front of a mirror. During the meeting, you present confidently, feeling good about your preparation. But as you wrap up, your supervisor leans forward and says, "I think this could've been more detailed. It felt a bit surface-level for this group."

The words hit you like a punch in the gut. Your face flushes with embarrassment, your heart quickens, and suddenly your mind is flooded with what Dr. Daniel Amen calls "ANTs"—automatic negative thoughts. "He doesn't think I'm smart enough. I worked so hard—why does it feel like that doesn't matter?" These intrusive thoughts spiral quickly, and your instinct might be to shut down completely or jump into defensive mode.

It takes practice, but we've seen critical words that initially sting turn into nutrient-dense fertilizer that produces beautiful fruit. The key is to respond instead of react.

Rather than letting automatic thoughts take control when you feel triggered, you can tell yourself to stay calm, take a breath, and ask for clarity. You might say, "Thanks for that feedback. Could you share which parts you felt needed more depth? I want to make sure it's thorough enough next time." This simple shift from reacting to responding transforms a potentially damaging moment into an opportunity for growth and connection.

The Impact of Doing the Internal Work

Year 2 shifts focus from inner work to outer impact. Leaders who've done the foundational work of understanding their patterns and triggers are now ready to unlock potential in others through feedback and coaching.

Whether you realize it or not, every interaction is either unlocking potential or limiting it. There is no neutral. Your ability to develop others is directly connected to your willingness to develop yourself.

Many leaders avoid the hard conversations needed for growth—with their teams and with themselves. They hesitate to give direct feedback, struggle with status updates, or dance around performance issues. This avoidance creates exactly what they're trying to prevent: defensive team members, missed deadlines, and constant firefighting.

One of Isaiah's clients, a 28-year-old marketing director at a commercial real estate company, was stepping into her first leadership role with her company. She was smart and capable, but giving feedback or asking for status updates made her uncomfortable. She hesitated to follow up because her team often got defensive. As a result, projects often slipped through the cracks.

Then, she started using the Bloom system.

After a few months, here's what she said:

"The weekly meetings and the shared priorities have changed everything. Now when I ask how something's going, it doesn't feel like I'm singling someone out. It's just part of how we work. People aren't defensive anymore. I can actually lead."

With Bloom, she needed fewer one-on-ones. Within the first quarter, she was putting out fewer fires. A streamlined system for managing progress ensured her team started delivering marketing materials on time—and without all the stress.

She didn't have to become more assertive or change her personality. The system gave her a structure that made leadership feel natural and effective.

For new managers, conflict avoiders, or anyone who struggles with managing personalities, this kind of structure is a lifesaver. It makes room for honest, candid conversations without putting people on the defensive.

When Leaders Bloom, Everyone Flourishes

The Relationship Curriculum delivers life-changing epiphanies. Leaders gain powerful insight into how they relate to themselves and to others, uncovering blind spots and patterns that have quietly shaped their behavior for years. These aren't surface-level insights. This is deep, personal growth that ripples across teams, fueling stronger relationships, more trust, and a culture where transformation isn't just possible—it's inevitable.

When leadership teams commit to transforming how they work together, that shift cascades through every department and relationship in the organization. Customers feel it in the consistency and quality of service. Vendors experience it in clearer communication and stronger partnerships. Employees see it in better decision-making and more effective collaboration.

This isn't just about better strategy or sharper execution—it's about building a company where relationships drive results, where trust accelerates growth, and where the leadership team's transformation becomes the catalyst for organization-wide success.

The Relationship Curriculum creates leaders who can do both: leaders who know themselves deeply and can create the conditions for others to flourish. They become architects of human potential because they've first learned to architect their own.

We've seen leaders who go through this journey transform how they show up for themselves first. Then they transform their team. When the team transforms, the entire organization blooms. The clients and the communities they serve are impacted in a positive way. The effects are profound and limitless.

An $80M Company on the Brink of Financial Collapse Transformed by Vulnerability

Cesar Quintero became a Coach Community Leader to Latin America after building his own successful businesses and discovering a passion for helping entrepreneurs fall in love with their business again.

Working with an $80 million company where the two owners had been carrying enormous weight on their shoulders, I learned they were facing a $1 million loan payment that could endanger the entire company's future, and they'd been handling this crisis alone.

During our first offsite session together, something remarkable happened. These owners finally opened up to their leadership team about the loan crisis they were facing.

What happened next brought them to tears.

Instead of the panic or blame they'd expected, their entire team immediately aligned around one mission: do everything in their power to help make that payment on time. The relief was overwhelming. These two leaders realized their team genuinely wanted to help them succeed. And in just one quarter, by focusing on what mattered most and getting all teams and departments rowing in the same direction, they made the payment that once seemed impossible.

This is the isolation pattern I see repeatedly with business owners. We convince ourselves that we need to project confidence and shield our teams from uncertainty. But this approach backfires—it creates the very isolation we're trying to avoid.

Once the truth was out, everything changed. The team didn't just rally—they doubled their expected sales that quarter. Suddenly, everyone felt a sense of ownership they'd never experienced before. The vulnerability and openness allowed the owners to be truly seen by their people, and it unified everyone around a common goal.

Your team's future is tied to the business. They want to share the burden because they're invested too. When my clients' leadership team learned the stakes, they rallied immediately.

A year later, the transformation was remarkable. One of the partners is now taking a sabbatical trip around the world with his family while the team runs things, empowered by alignment and ownership.

Cesar Quintero,
Coach Community Leader, Latin America

The Launch
Bloom Days 1, 30, 60, & 90

"Small disciplines repeated with consistency every day lead to great achievements ... "

———————————————————— John Maxwell

"Success is a few simple disciplines, practiced every day; while failure is simply a few errors in judgment, repeated every day."

———————————————————— Jim Rohn

Bloom Day 1 | Creating Your Ideal Future

The Bloom Growth Journey is designed to guide owners and leadership teams through the next three to five years, and we kick it off with a 90-day transformation that blends deeper team alignment with tactical improvements. By Year 3, teams emerge with such enthusiasm and results that even owners who had envisioned an exit are deciding to stay.

Since 2011, on at least a dozen occasions, I have heard from business owners who completed a successful exit. During acquisition, they were told that they are the most cohesive, well-organized business the buyer had ever seen. That's the power of Bloom Growth.

You can't have everything all at once—faster growth, higher profitability, and more free time—but with the right approach, you absolutely can achieve it all. The Bloom Journey helps prioritize what matters most and systematically works toward that vision with intention and velocity.

This journey begins with a powerful premise: **This is the day we work together to co-create your ideal future to get everything you want out of your business.**

Your 5-Year Vision

The future you're building starts with Bloom Day 1. It begins the moment your team sits down with eyes open, laptops closed, and minds ready to imagine something bigger.

Most teams walk in with a mix of uncertainty, anticipation, and curiosity. Some are fired up to co-create a bold new vision. Others arrive more reserved—especially the pragmatic, data-driven leaders who've sat through planning sessions before. That's normal. Change doesn't happen all at once, and skepticism has a place at the table. What matters is that everyone shows up.

You might sense a quiet tension in the room. Leaders are thinking about the emails piling up, the client fires, the questions waiting back at the office. That awareness is a tell-tale sign that shows us where growth is needed—not in hustle or more hours, but in delegation, clarity, and focused priorities.

The Difference Is in the Details

For Bloom Day 1, there's minimal preparation required— just a welcome email requesting the team to complete a check-in questionnaire (which takes about 10 minutes of thoughtful time) and bring an object representing a proud life moment. No extensive pre-reading. No heavy prep packet. Just that brief check-in—and a commitment to show up real, honest, and focused.

And when the most senior leaders model staying present and being vulnerable, the rest of the team follows. That creates the kind of trust and openness that drives meaningful change.

Taking time to make time is what turns success into scalability. To some, setting aside the time to create structure and align as a leadership team might feel like taking a step back, when, in fact, that step propels you forward with clarity and momentum.

In his *New York Times* bestseller, *Atomic Habits*, James Clear writes about how we can harness the power of small habits to create big changes. He shares an example of the British cycling team taking the Tour de France by storm after David Brailsford came on as the team's new Performance Director.

With Brailsford's "marginal gains" philosophy, the team went from a 100-year history of zero championships and only one Olympic medal to multiple Tour de France victories, setting both world records and Olympic records, and capturing Olympic gold medals by the dozens. All within a 10-year span of focusing on tiny 1% improvements—seemingly marginal gains. But those small improvements added up, creating an outcome that made cycling history.

Small improvements can have a big impact.

Yes, there's often resistance. "*I can't be offline all day.*" "*My team needs me.*" Yet, by the end of the session, those same leaders realize:

"Time spent on strategy buys back time for execution."

As Bloom takes root, they become more present and more effective—without being constantly tethered to their phones. To make this possible, Bloom Day 1—and every session after—is held off site, away from workplace distractions. Everyone arrives early. The agenda is clear: this is the most valuable work they will do for their business that day, and it requires their full attention.

Creating a physical space that's conducive to a successful off-site planning session is imperative.

The room should be:

- Quiet, with natural light and functional HVAC
- Equipped with a large whiteboard and a screen for easy laptop connectivity
- Stocked with accessible outlets and comfortable seating
- Arranged with a round table or, at minimum, a square or U-shape configuration so the team is seated as equals (long rectangular tables are the worst)
- Free of clutter and distractions

It should also offer basic comforts that support focus and flow:

- A reliable coffee machine, tea station, and water dispenser
- Nearby restrooms
- Privacy for honest conversations
- Healthy lunch delivery to minimize disruption and maximize energy
- Easy access to supplies like pens and a printer
- Secure WiFi

Designating a point person to handle logistics and lunch orders prevents unnecessary distractions. And proximity matters—teams are more present when they don't need to trek across a building for coffee or a bathroom break.

These little conveniences help keep the team engaged, energized, and in the zone—especially during breaks and mealtimes, where some of the best side conversations happen.

Starting Small

On Day 1, the smallest version of the leadership team gathers together. This is going to be anywhere from three to seven people. We strongly recommend not bringing in more than seven leaders to start the Bloom Growth Journey. The best practice is to start lean and gradually expand.

Some members instantly see the possibilities while others need space to think it through. That range of perspective isn't a barrier—it's a strength. The Bloom Growth Journey is built to unify diverse viewpoints into one aligned path forward.

One of the first breakthroughs comes when we tackle "visionary whiplash"—that constant rush of exciting ideas rarely seen through to completion. Our coaches specialize in helping visionaries channel their boundless creativity, providing the focus and structure needed to prevent constant pivots from creating chaos for the team.

As we capture all the team's Opportunities and Obstacles (O&Os) and start organizing them into something usable, we'll refine them into Quarterly Priorities (QPs), you can almost hear the collective exhale:

"We finally get to focus. We know what matters for the next 90 days. We can actually finish."

This direct guidance ensures that big ideas are not only captured but also executed, fostering the stability and trust that allows teams to thrive. And that shift—from scattered to strategic—is powerful.

Laying the Foundation for Growth

From there, we introduce the **Ideal Leadership Team Structure**—not a theoretical organization chart, but a living blueprint for sustainable growth. Gaps are revealed. Root issues come into focus. Team members learn new things about each other, even after years of working together.

By the end of Day 1, your team walks away with:

- Clear, focused 90-day priorities
- Shared alignment on how you'll grow—and why it matters
- A blueprint of your ideal leadership structure
- A deeper bond and connection as a team

The real transformation, however, unfolds in the weeks—and years—that follow.

Your Bloom Growth Coach stays with you, guiding implementation, holding space, and asking the right questions. Because at Bloom, we don't come with answers—we come with *better questions*. The wisdom is already in the room. A coach's job is to help your team unlock it.

NOTE: If any of these concepts are new or unfamiliar, check out the Glossary of Terms at the back of this book. There's also a 5-page TL;DR (too long; didn't read) summary for those who like to skip to the end.

Building Deeper Bonds

From the very first off-site session, we introduce something that might feel unexpected in a business setting: exercises designed to help leadership teams connect on a deeper level. When leaders genuinely know and trust each other, they make better decisions faster, communicate more directly, and create the kind of culture that attracts and retains top talent.

The science backs this up. Teams with high psychological safety—where people feel comfortable being vulnerable and authentic—consistently outperform others. They're more creative, more resilient, and more willing to take the calculated risks that fuel growth.

The challenge is that most leadership teams operate at the surface level. They know each other's professional strengths but not their personal motivations. They can debate strategy but avoid honest conversations about performance or concerns. They maintain politeness without creating real connection.

That's why we start Day 1 with conversations that help leaders see each other as whole people, not just business roles. When a CFO understands what drives the CEO beyond financial metrics, or when a VP of Sales knows what matters most to the Operations Director outside of work, collaboration changes. Leaders extend grace when things get tough. They communicate with more context and empathy.

One thing that sets Bloom Growth OS apart from other operating systems is our intentional focus on human flourishing and elevated relationships. As Jim Kwik, author of *Limitless*, often puts it, "Whatever we nourish will flourish." We believe that when leaders invest in stronger relationships, those connections ripple outward—transforming the entire company.

The bonds built on Day 1 become the foundation for everything else. With deeper trust, leaders are more open to feedback, more candid about challenges, and more committed to collective success over individual wins.

Here's a real example ... At an oil and gas company in Houston, four men in their late 30s to early 50s went through the "Deeper Bond" exercise with their Bloom Growth Coach, Jeremy Giroir. Jeremy admitted later: "If you told me five years ago that I'd be guiding oilmen through breathing exercises to help them talk about their feelings, I would have said you were crazy!"

But that's exactly what happened. He began by explaining how trust improves team performance, then led them through a simple breathing exercise and a guided conversation. "Simply by doing our breathing exercise together, the mood in the room changed," Jeremy recalled. Even though the team was doubtful at first, they felt calmer and more relaxed after just a few minutes.

Next, each leader shared an object that represented something they were most proud of in their lives. For the first time, they opened up and shared personal stories they had never talked about at work. The impact was immediate. At the end of the session, the "burliest" team member said it was the best part of his day. He admitted that although he worked with one of the owners every day, he had never even seen pictures of that owner's children until then.

For businesses that want to grow and endure, these stronger personal connections are essential. At Bloom, we know that sustainable success is rooted in healthy relationships—with your team, your clients, and yourself. That's why we weave our Relationship Curriculum into every session.

When leaders deepen trust, resolve tension, and strengthen culture, everything else starts to flow. Performance improves, creativity opens up, and the team genuinely enjoys working together.

Outcomes | Day 1

1. Clarity through prioritization. Focus areas become sharper and more actionable.
2. A sense of structure. Initial alignment around leadership roles and organizational dynamics.
3. Consistent communication. The Bloom Weekly meeting establishes a reliable rhythm for staying aligned, tracking progress, and addressing opportunities and obstacles proactively.
4. Stronger team connections. Participants feel honored to be part of the strategic conversation—often for the first time.

Key Activities | Day 1

- **Co-Create a 5-Year Vision.** Dream big together so the whole leadership team is building toward the same exciting future from Day 1.
- **Establish Quarterly Priorities.** Turn all those great ideas into clear, achievable 90-day goals, so the team can actually focus on what matters and finish what they start.

- **Design the Ideal Leadership Team Structure.** Create an initial draft of the ideal leadership team structure to grow into over the next 12 months.
- **Deeper Bond Conversation.** Strengthen team trust and personal connections through activities that encourage leaders to open up and share.
- **Train and Launch the Bloom Weekly Meeting.** Create a cadence of consistent communication to stay on track from Day 1.

Bloom Day 30 | Transformation Takes Root

By Day 30, leadership teams have been running Bloom Weekly meetings and are beginning to see improvements on their communication and execution as a team. They have tangible proof of their progress because it's automatically tracked by the software.

Once they've had a couple calls with their Growth Coach and started working on their Quarterly Priorities (90-day goals), we start hearing things like, "Oh, this is so much better than what we were doing before."

The excitement about the 5-Year Vision starts to take hold. There's this realization that they're working toward something *bigger and better* than they ever thought possible. Things crystallize and the team begins to see a clear destination for where the organization is headed.

Teams come into their offsite meeting excited and optimistic about what they're going to do with their coach— partly because of the new and innovative things they did on the first day and partly because they're beginning to see progress.

It's true what Napoleon Hill wrote in *Think and Grow Rich* about harnessing your thoughts to shape your reality: "Whatever the mind of man can conceive and believe, it can achieve."

Aligning Heads and Hearts

If we asked 20 people in your company what you do, how many different answers would we get?" If the response is "10 different answers," that's a strong sign that your business lacks alignment.

Clearly articulating what you do in a way that's raw, real, gritty, and authentic is an opportunity filter for deciding which growth opportunities to target and which ones to discard.

Is the entire organization truly connected with the company's purpose? You'll only find out if you take the time to get clear on each individual "*Why*" and the organization's deeper purpose.

For example, one of our clients generates revenue by exporting seafood, but their deeper purpose is to provide jobs and stimulate economic growth in Latin America with thousands of local fishermen and their families.

One of the first steps in getting an organization fully dialed in is creating clarity around *What* you do, *How* you do it, and *Why* it matters. When these three essentials are clear, the entire team moves in sync—heads and hearts aligned.

Unleashing Positive Energy

We all create stories about our teammates, our direct reports, and our leadership—stories that become mental traps. Someone asks you to document a conversation, and suddenly you're convinced you're about to be fired. A colleague seems distant in a meeting, and you decide they're undermining your project. These relationship narratives drain massive amounts of energy. You're not just doing your job—you're managing an entire fictional storyline about what everyone else is thinking or planning.

The impact of the Relationship Curriculum is that it frees up this energy—energy that was previously tied up in drama, friction, limiting beliefs, or old stories we've been telling ourselves. Sometimes we're stuck in patterns or traps we don't even realize we're in.

Each session, when we come together, helps surface these patterns. We draw them out, look at them, and once they're addressed—and we actually do something about them—it's as though someone just removed a 50-pound weight from their shoulders. When teams learn to validate assumptions instead of creating stories, that mental bandwidth gets redirected toward actual productivity.

That has a direct effect on how productive we are as a team and, honestly, how much fun we're having while working together. That's the part I really love.

Metrics: The Power of Simplicity

One of the first steps we take is clarifying the targets. What are the key metrics that truly matter to your business?

Too often, companies either drown in endless data or run on instinct alone, disconnected from the financial pulse of the business.

Our approach is to simplify. We identify the most important numbers and the actions that drive them, then break those actions into weekly steps that both produce and predict your financial outcomes. The goal isn't to collect data for its own sake—it's to get the right data at the right time so you can make proactive decisions.

When chosen well, weekly KPIs bridge the gap between your long-term vision (your 90-day, 1-year, and 3-year Growth Goals) and the day-to-day work of your team. They become levers you can actually control, forecasting problems before they escalate and highlighting opportunities as they emerge.

Defining the right metrics isn't always quick (it might take an hour or it might take a year) but once in place, they give you clarity and direction. You're no longer blindsided by the numbers. Nail the right metrics each week, and success follows.

KPIs as Predictors, Not Just Results

Most leaders think about metrics as results, but the real power comes from measuring the activities that lead to results. Done right, predictive KPIs give you confidence that the right actions are being taken each week—actions that drive the outcomes you want at the end of the quarter.

Sales and marketing provide the clearest examples. Of course, every department has KPIs, but sales and marketing are the easiest to understand and quantify, so we often start there. How many outreach attempts were made this week? How many first calls or meaningful meetings took place? These are leading indicators of future sales.

It's not enough to track deals closed—especially if your sales cycle takes months. If it takes six months to close a deal, waiting on closed sales means you're always six months behind. Instead, you need metrics that forecast the future. For instance, if outbound calls dip today, you know sales will dip months from now. Predictive metrics give you the chance to solve the problem now—before it grows into a crisis.

That's the real value: tracking early activities so that by the time sales are measured, you've already built momentum instead of scrambling to catch up.

Letters from Your Future Self

One powerful exercise in the Relationship Curriculum asks each leadership team member to envision who they're going to become as a leader over the next five years—then write it down in detail and share it with their team.

Most people never think deeply about their future self like this. But here's what happens when they do: their brain processes this vision three distinct times—first when they imagine it, again when they write it down, and a third time when they share it out loud. Each step drives it deeper into their psyche and subconscious, dramatically increasing the likelihood they'll actually become that leader.

The letters are always inspiring. Leaders paint vivid pictures of their growth, their impact, and the person they've evolved into. After each person reads their letter, the coach asks a simple question:

"What component of the leader you've described could we support you in becoming right now—this year?"

Research shows that goals shared with people you respect have exponentially higher success rates. When you commit to your future vision with your leadership team, you've created accountability that pulls you forward—especially when things get tough and you're tempted to settle for less than your best.

What started as individual reflection transforms into collective commitment to help each member step closer to their future self today. It's beautiful to watch the leadership team become invested in each other's growth journey.

Outcomes | Day 30

1. Growth is simplified by identifying the weekly actions that drive results. Teams move from being overwhelmed by data or disconnected from their numbers to having clear KPIs that predict future outcomes and enable proactive decision-making.
2. Leadership teams are having the best, most productive weekly meetings they've ever experienced. Communication and execution improve dramatically with tangible proof of progress automatically tracked by the software.
3. Authentic alignment around the *What, How,* and *Why.* Teams achieve head-and-heart connection through clarified purpose and a shared "why."

4. Mental energy is freed up for actual productivity. Leaders begin identifying the negative stories that have been draining their energy, redirecting that bandwidth toward getting real work done.
5. The 5-Year Vision becomes clearer and feels achievable. Teams shift from day-to-day survival mode to excitement about working toward something bigger and better than they ever thought possible.

Key Activities | Day 30

- **Write Letter from Your Future Self.** Visualize who you will become over the next five years, write it down in detail, and share it with the team.
- **Rewrite Your Internal Dialogue.** Bring awareness to negative narratives and reframe the stories that may be holding you back.
- **Focus Only on Important Metrics.** Simplify your Growth Goals and weekly KPIs to understand the actions that actually move those numbers.
- **Track What Predicts Success.** Monitor weekly activities like calls, meetings, and outreach that predict future wins rather than just measuring results.
- **Align Heads and Hearts.** Help teams articulate their *What*, *How*, and *Why* to ensure everyone works toward the same company purpose.

Bloom Day 60 | Bridging the Present to the Future

By Day 60, teams walk into the room with a completely different energy. They're not wondering what comes next, they're aligned, focused, and genuinely excited to be working together.

This is when we hear things like, "I finally see how everything connects," and "We're not just busy anymore—we're actually building something." The skeptic who's been quietly wondering if all this effort is worth it? They're the ones who often have the biggest "aha" moments.

Here's what's happening: We've bridged the gap between their big 5-Year Vision and what they're doing today. For the first time, they can see their roadmap for growth—not just wishful thinking, but a clear, practical path forward.

By Day 60, leaders are reallocating their time to higher-value activities instead of getting stuck in the same old patterns. The team has moved from reactive to strategic, from frustrated to focused. They're not just working harder—they're working on what actually matters.

Vision and Goals

On Day 60, the coach leads the team in creating their 3-Year Future and Annual Goals. This bridges the gap between the 90-day sprint you're currently in and the aspirational 5-Year Vision you established on Day 1.

The 3-Year Future serves as your mid-range target—close enough to feel tangible, far enough to be transformational. Teams often find this timeframe perfect for planning major initiatives like geographic expansion, new product launches, or significant operational upgrades. While five years can feel abstract, three years is concrete enough to drive real planning and commitment.

Annual Goals translate that 3-Year Future into immediate action. These aren't wish lists or vague intentions—they're specific, measurable outcomes that will move you meaningfully closer to your vision. Teams typically set 4-7 Annual Goals that balance growth initiatives with operational improvements.

The power of this cascading timeline—from 5 years to 3 years to 1 year to 90 days—creates momentum at every level. Your team can see exactly how today's work connects to tomorrow's vision. When someone questions whether a project is worth pursuing, you have a clear framework for evaluation: Does this move us toward our 3-Year Future?

After completing Day 60, teams consistently report a shift in energy. The excitement is palpable because everyone can see the path forward. Abstract vision becomes concrete strategy. Hope transforms into planning. The roadmap isn't just clearer—it's actionable, and everyone knows their part in making it real.

Core Values Discovery

All organizations have core values, but only about half have them clearly defined. We excavate for these values, which have always been true of your organization and continue to be true. We have you describe them in the simplest way possible, so your core values can be used as people filters for hiring, firing, reviews, rewards, and recognition.

This discovery process uncovers what's at the heart of the organization. Core values are essentially characteristics of being human. Our personal core values reflect who we strive to be as human beings—they represent our best selves. Likewise, an organization's core values represent how that business shows up in the world. These aren't new aspirations or fresh ideals—they're the timeless principles that have been consistently present throughout your organization's journey.

Whether we're consciously aware of this or not, all decision making comes from shared core values. Finding clients, customers, and employees can feel overwhelming because there are so many options. But clearly defined values act as a filter for working with customers, vendors, and teammates who share similar characteristics. These values are non-negotiable for anyone to be in a relationship with your business. When you stay aligned with who you really are and don't compromise for profit or to please others, the right answer becomes clear. It's one decision that makes a thousand others.

The Personal Energy Audit

During your Day 60 offsite planning session, your Growth Coach will guide you through what we call a "personal energy audit"—an exercise that consistently produces some of the most eye-opening moments in the Bloom Growth Journey. This simple but revealing process examines the often startling gap between what you say your priorities are and where you actually invest your time and energy.

The audit itself is straightforward: you'll identify your top professional priorities and then examine your calendar from the past month to see where your time really went. More importantly, you'll identify the tasks that are low value and drain your energy, then make concrete decisions about which ones to stop doing entirely, which ones to automate, and which ones to delegate (stop/automate/ delegate = SAD). But don't let the simplicity fool you—this exercise has the power to fundamentally shift how you think about your role as a strategic leader and your approach to allocating your time.

The results are remarkably consistent across industries and leadership levels. Most leaders find that 60–80% of their time is spent on activities that don't align with their stated priorities. They discover they're buried in operational details while their strategic priorities remain neglected. They realize they're attending meetings where their presence adds little value while the high-impact work that only they can do sits on the back burner.

This isn't a time management problem—it's a delegation and trust problem. When leaders haven't built the systems and relationships that enable their teams to execute independently, they become bottlenecks rather than accelerators; we often say the bottleneck is at the top of the bottle (organization). The energy audit illuminates this dynamic with uncomfortable clarity.

What makes this exercise so powerful is the moment of recognition it creates. Leaders often describe it as simultaneously deflating and energizing—deflating because they see how far their actual behavior has drifted from their stated intentions and energizing because they suddenly have a clear roadmap for change.

The audit reveals a fundamental leadership truth: your willingness to delegate operational excellence directly correlates with your ability to focus on strategic leadership. Every hour spent on work that someone else could handle at 80% quality is an hour forfeited from engaging in the strategic work that only you can do at 100% quality.

Your Growth Coach will help you process these insights and make the critical decisions: What low-value, energy-draining tasks will you stop doing completely? Which repetitive processes can be automated? And what responsibilities are you ready to delegate to develop your team's capabilities? This systematic approach to stopping (or "strategic quitting," if you prefer), automating, and delegating creates space for the high-impact leadership work that only you can do. It's where the real work of leadership transformation begins.

Breaking Free from Limiting Beliefs

Days 30–60 are when the deeper work begins—identifying and addressing the limiting beliefs and fictional storylines that drain energy. Leaders operate from beliefs they don't even realize they have. They assume their team can't handle bigger challenges, so they hold onto tasks instead of empowering others. They believe difficult conversations will damage relationships, so they avoid them entirely. When a direct report seems overwhelmed, they take work back instead of asking what support is needed. When a team member stays quiet in meetings, they assume disengagement instead of recognizing different processing styles.

These unconscious assumptions create the very problems leaders are trying to improve. Holding onto work that stems from "they can't handle this" actually prevents people from stepping up and growing. Conflict avoidance that comes from "this will hurt our relationship" lets small issues fester into major dysfunction.

Day 60 requires teams to confront these relationship traps (the limiting beliefs holding them back). The work is uncomfortable, yet this is exactly where breakthrough happens. As these invisible chains fall away, each member of the leadership team discovers energy that had been trapped in unconscious assumptions and limiting beliefs, enabling them to create new response patterns that unlock team potential and redirect mental bandwidth toward higher-value activities.

When leaders stop operating from limiting beliefs about themselves, their people, and their situations, teams unlock potential they didn't even know existed.

The transformation is profound. Clear thinking drives confident action, which naturally lifts both team spirit and performance. Leaders who once hesitated now delegate with confidence. Teams that avoided tough conversations now tackle them head-on. The energy previously consumed by unhelpful narratives flows into innovation, problem-solving, and genuine connection.

Outcomes | Day 60

1. Leaders gain awareness of what energy needs to be reallocated to higher-value tasks.
2. The team gains a clear roadmap for future growth through Annual Goal-setting and the creation of their 3-Year Future.
3. Core Values Discovery acts as a people filter for choosing employees, customers, and vendors.

Key Activities | Day 60

- **Complete Personal Energy Audit.** Identify low-value, energy-draining tasks and decide to stop, automate, or delegate them.

- **Identify Relationship Traps.** Address limiting beliefs and create new response patterns that unlock team potential and redirect focus.
- **Map Out the Future.** Set clear 3-Year Goals and Annual Goals that connect daily work to the big 5-Year Vision.

Bloom Day 90 | Integrating the Transformation

By Day 90, the leadership team is ready for a shift. Up to now, they've been carrying the weight of the entire business on their shoulders, and they're eager to share this process with their respective teams. When that happens, the weight gets redistributed and the potential energy multiplies.

After 90 days of transformation, leaders look around and think, "How did we ever function before this?"

The whole purpose of Day 90 is to crystallize, refine, and polish the work leading up to now. It's a big day. The excitement builds as the leadership team prepares to lead their own departments through this next phase, getting ready to unleash the Growth Plan across the entire organization.

Finalizing the Foundation

Day 90 marks a critical transition point. The leadership team has spent three months working exclusively together, building trust, aligning on vision, and learning the system. Now it's time to finalize the foundational elements that will guide the entire organization forward.

This includes polishing the Growth Plan until it's crystal clear, ensuring Core Values are defined with supporting stories that bring them to life, and crafting key messages that will resonate throughout the company. Every element needs to be ready for prime time because after today, it all goes company-wide.

The Leadership Transformation

After a quarter or two, leaders will often say that they're getting more time back, feeling less overwhelmed, and witnessing more predictable business results. This brings unexpected relief for those who've been grinding for so long. The shift from being the bottleneck to being the multiplier is profound.

Leaders report hearing their teams say things like, "I can't believe how much easier this feels," and "My team is solving problems I used to lose sleep over." This transformation occurs because tactical decision-making shifts to those closest to the action, leading to better, faster decisions while freeing the leadership team to rise into truly strategic roles.

Rolling Out to Departments

Shortly after Day 90, the leadership team becomes the teacher. They roll out their own abbreviated Day 1 experience to each department with weekly execution rhythms. The key advantage is that they facilitate each other's department planning sessions, creating cross-functional collaboration that breaks down silos.

Each department leader guides their team through setting department-specific KPIs, clarifying their org chart, and launching their own Bloom Weekly meetings. Now you have three, four, maybe five departments all running the same playbook, all moving in the same direction. The energy multiplies exponentially.

Department teams take ownership of problems they used to escalate, developing the autonomy and proactive problem-solving that drives real transformation.

The All-Organization Launch

The culmination of Day 90 is preparing for the all-company meeting that follows. This is where the entire organization comes together to hear the refined Growth Plan, understand the Core Values with real stories that illustrate them, and see how every person fits into the bigger picture.

The leadership team crafts these messages carefully, ensuring they're clear, inspiring, and actionable. They prepare Core Values stories that showcase real examples of these values in action. They practice presenting the Growth Plan in a way that helps every employee see their role in achieving it.

This all-organization gathering transforms abstract concepts into shared reality. When everyone hears the same message at the same time, alignment accelerates dramatically.

The Ongoing Rhythm

After Day 90, teams launch into a 5-day per year rhythm, meeting with their Growth Coach one full day per quarter and two full days for annual planning. Every 90 days, they reconvene to reset, reevaluate, and learn additional tools. This is the rhythm that drives transformation.

Integral to this ongoing rhythm is the continued integration of the Relationship Curriculum. Each session builds upon the last, fostering deeper self-awareness, emotional intelligence, and stronger interpersonal connections within the leadership team.

The Growth Coach provides the agendas while the software supports execution and communication, helping to ensure progress remains on track with ongoing mentorship. At this point, the leadership team moves from being students to becoming leaders and trainers of the Bloom Growth OS.

Exponential Impact

You've already got your core players performing optimally and they're ready to roll this out department-wide. Until now, it's been three to seven people. Suddenly, it's 15 to 25. Going from three to seven people aligned and executing well to 15 to 25 people creates massive engagement across the entire business.

It's a dual focus that compounds over time: stronger business systems paired with stronger leadership capabilities. Because both are improving simultaneously, the results are exponential.

The first 90 days establish a framework for transformation. By aligning tactical execution with strategic vision and personal growth, companies emerge stronger, more cohesive, and primed for sustained success. The real win is a team that's not just working together, but flourishing together.

Outcomes | Day 90

1. Leadership teams move from iterating to executing with certainty and excitement about the path forward.
2. Complete leadership buy-in creates a unified Growth Plan the entire organization is ready to follow.
3. A clear, repeatable cadence ensures continued momentum beyond the initial 90 days.

Key Activities | Day 90

- **Leaders Become Trainers.** Transition the leadership team from students to coaches, guiding their departments through goal setting and weekly meetings.
- **Launch Department-Level Implementation.** Expand the Growth Plan beyond leadership with each department starting their own Bloom Journey and execution meetings.
- **Complete System Mastery Training.** Prepare leaders with comprehensive coaching skills to run the new system effectively with their teams.
- **Scale Company-Wide Rollout.** Finalize and unveil the Growth Plan across all departments to multiply engagement and operational excellence.

The Bloom Launch

The first 90 days lays the foundation for your growth using Bloom, from the 90-Minute Discovery Meeting to Bloom Days 1, 30, 60, and 90. This graphic summarizes the launch of the Bloom Journey:

START

90-Minute Discovery Meeting
Bring together the Entrepreneur and the smallest version of the Leadership Team to determine if the Bloom Growth Operating System (BGOS) is the right fit for their business.

DAY 01

Foundation & Vision
Develop future structure, 5-Year Vision, Quarterly Priorities, and operational meeting cadence to drive sustained execution and team cohesion.

DAY 30

Performance & Communication
Establish weekly KPI tracking system and strategic framework (What, How, Why) to drive measurable progress toward 3-Year, 1-Year, and 90-Day goals.

DAY 60

Purpose & Potential
Define core values, 3-Year Vision, and annual goals while implementing relationship management and energy optimization frameworks for enhanced team performance.

DAY 90

Integration & Scale
Complete quarterly review, set new priorities, finalize comprehensive Growth Plan, and commit to cascading the operating system across the organization.

—————— Bloom Year 1
Building the Foundation for Sustainable Growth

"You do not rise to the level of your goals. You fall to the level of your systems."

—————— James Clear, *Atomic Habits*

"Habits are the invisible architecture of everyday life."

—————— Gretchen Rubin, *Better Than Before*

Team Clarity Comes First

In the first 90 days, we don't rush to change anything. There's space to reflect, explore ideas, and begin to align around the 5-Year Vision. The goal isn't immediate action—it's clarity. That clarity is gold. It becomes the launchpad for every major decision that follows.

There are a dozen connections with the coach per year, including five off-site sessions, meeting one full day per quarter and two full days for annual planning. By the end of Day 90, leadership teams begin to see the landscape clearly. They start to identify where they are stuck, and then the confluence of Quarterly Priorities (goals), KPIs, Process, and decisive people moves combines to unlock the pent-up potential. Your business does have pent-up potential—I've never met an entrepreneur who doesn't. I have met many entrepreneurs and their teams unwilling to do the work or follow a process, and they remain stuck.

One thing becomes obvious fast: The right leadership team is everything. Most businesses start Year 1 focused on exactly that—getting the right people in the right seats. That doesn't necessarily mean replacing people. Often, it's simply aligning roles to match the future the business is building.

Sometimes that means recognizing a gap and hiring for a role that's never existed—like a full-time marketing leader. Sometimes it means shifting from outsourced financial support to an in-house strategic partner. Often, it's splitting one overloaded role into two. These are strategic, future-focused people moves. On average, we recommend making only one significant leadership shift per quarter.

My client who went from a $45 million valuation to $215 million in just over five years (after 70 years in business)—remember what they said made the biggest difference?

"It was getting the right people in the right seats on the leadership team."

That team built everything else.

Staying Focused on the Future

A team that is aligned and laser-focused on their ideal future is unstoppable. They're not bouncing from idea to idea, shiny object to shiny object. They stay with the challenge, quarter after quarter, trying different approaches until it's resolved.

A founder might've once tackled a problem for 60 days and moved on without fully solving the root cause. But now there's a team focused on the long game. They identify their opportunities and obstacles. They remove the friction, lean into what's working, and build from there.

If they try one approach and it doesn't work, they try again next quarter. And the next. They're persistent about solving issues in a permanent and inspiring way—because they know what they're building and they know what's in the way.

Bloom Strategic Offsite Rhythm

Each year, the leadership team and Bloom Growth Coach gather for three full-day offsite Bloom Quarterly planning sessions and a two-day for the Bloom Annual as outlined by the graphic below:

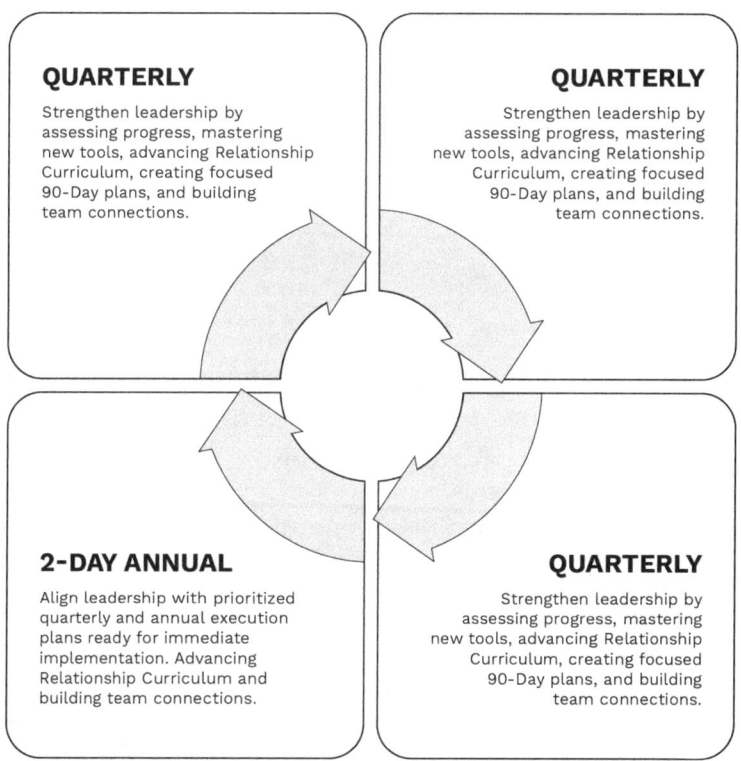

QUARTERLY

Strengthen leadership by assessing progress, mastering new tools, advancing Relationship Curriculum, creating focused 90-Day plans, and building team connections.

QUARTERLY

Strengthen leadership by assessing progress, mastering new tools, advancing Relationship Curriculum, creating focused 90-Day plans, and building team connections.

2-DAY ANNUAL

Align leadership with prioritized quarterly and annual execution plans ready for immediate implementation. Advancing Relationship Curriculum and building team connections.

QUARTERLY

Strengthen leadership by assessing progress, mastering new tools, advancing Relationship Curriculum, creating focused 90-Day plans, and building team connections.

True Organizational Alignment

As the leadership team levels up, the ripple effects move through the next layer of the business. This is where most companies hit a ceiling. Even with a clear vision, departmental silos or misaligned goals can pull energy away from what's best for the whole.

It's not conscious malice—nobody shows up saying they're going to hurt the business today. But they often unconsciously prioritize either their team's or their own interests over the organization's.

What's needed is 100% of employees and teammates all aligned around the organization's best interest, trusting that as the organization wins, each individual team member also wins.

There's no way to be operating in your own self-interest or your department's self-interest and have the whole organization win. You have to be aligned with the greater good of the whole.

When trust is built and alignment grows, everything changes. Drama disappears. Defensiveness fades. Politics go out the window. In their place, you'll find focus, freedom, fun, flow, and forward motion.

We've seen it time and time again. A group of individuals becomes a unified force. They know their purpose. They're connected to their "why." And they move together—with speed, with honesty, and without ego.

This kind of alignment is rare—but not because it's impossible. Most businesses just haven't had the structure or support to create it. But once it clicks, it's electric.

The Execution and Communication System Emerges

The first year of transformation includes both exciting wins and challenging obstacles. It's messy, it's unpredictable, and it requires patience. And it's when you begin to see glimpses of your future reality.

The focus isn't on immediate results but on creating sustainable systems. The foundation you build this year will support your company's growth trajectory for the long term.

What makes this year so critical is that you're simultaneously working on multiple fronts. You're getting the right people in the right seats, building your dream leadership team for the next level. You're identifying where your business is stuck—those process breakdowns, leadership gaps, or operational constraints that have been holding you back. And you're implementing the systems that will create the foundation for everything that follows.

The beauty of this approach is that momentum builds on itself. As you resolve one stuck point, it unlocks another area of growth. As your team gets stronger, they can handle more complex challenges. As your communication rhythms improve, decision-making gets faster and more effective.

By the end of Year 1, you're not just running a better business—you're running a business that's positioned to scale without breaking down. And a whole new realm of possibilities opens up.

Creating a Consistent Cadence

Transformation begins with the leadership team implementing weekly leadership meetings on Day 1, what we call the "Bloom Weekly" (BW). This weekly cadence becomes a complete game changer. Even clients who've worked with their coach for three or four years say that their Bloom Weekly is still one of the most brilliant parts of how their teams operate.

Beyond the initial leadership work, quarterly one-on-one coaching conversations happen between every boss and employee. These aren't reviews; they're vital coaching and alignment opportunities, supported by agendas within the software.

With the support of their coach, teams are guided through process mapping, where they clarify their top five to seven meaningful business processes—who owns each one, the agreed-upon timeline for each step, and the desired outcome.

In addition to a clear desired outcome, teams can identify speed and quality measurements throughout their processes, unlocking significant continuous improvement opportunities. This ensures everyone aligns on handling recurring tasks, onboarding, and training, providing clarity for consistent execution.

Financial transparency also becomes a focus, with teams learning to run monthly profit and loss (P&L) meetings using a dedicated agenda. This ensures the leadership team has a crystal-clear, simple grasp of the business's financial levers.

Throughout this entire process, your Growth Coach offers guidance as the team launches critical, practical tools to help make better decisions and keep everyone aligned. Clear agendas and structure ensure these crucial new habits take hold, which is at the heart of sustainable growth.

From Leadership Mastery to Organization-Wide Impact

Starting at Day 90, leaders are trained to facilitate compelling organization-wide meetings that enroll employees across all departments in achieving the Growth Plan. While you'll see results immediately after Day 1, organizational transformation requires time and consistency to create lasting change.

The leadership team masters the system first, typically needing three to six months to learn it well enough to teach the Bloom Weekly throughout the organization. Many teams find immediate results at this foundational level. After Day 90, the system expands to include everyone in their respective departments.

Once department-level Bloom Weekly meetings become operational, tactical decisions naturally flow to where they belong. Each department takes on more decision-making responsibility, allowing the leadership team to step into a truly strategic role while departments handle opportunities and obstacles at their source.

Every quarterly offsite throughout Year 1 follows a proven rhythm that maximizes both learning and execution. Roughly 60% of our energy focuses on what's working and what's not working with the business and the Bloom Growth Operating System itself.

Think of it like working with a skilled instructor. When you're learning a new yoga pose, small corrections in positioning can transform the entire experience—a slight shift in your foundation, a minor change in alignment, and suddenly you're accessing muscles and benefits you couldn't reach before. The same principle applies to a Growth OS.

With your coach's guidance, leadership teams make crucial refinements: tweaking processes that aren't flowing smoothly, course-correcting priorities that have drifted off track, and fine-tuning the system to match how your team actually works. The power lies in small, strategic shifts as opposed to major overhauls—modifications that unlock significant improvements in performance and clarity.

The remaining 40% of each offsite introduces new tools and creates experiences around the next steps of your Relationship Journey. This balance ensures teams are always building on a solid foundation while continuously expanding their capabilities.

Just like that instructor who spots the subtle changes that make all the difference, your Bloom Growth Coach sees what you can't see and guides you toward the refinements that will have the greatest impact on your team's effectiveness and growth.

Why External Guidance Matters

Bloom Growth Coaches aren't clairvoyant or smarter than leadership teams—they have the advantage of being seasoned entrepreneurs themselves and spending 60-120 days a year in the room with leadership teams. This creates powerful pattern recognition and clarity that's impossible to develop from the inside.

This external perspective explains why teams using a coach succeed with the Bloom Growth Operating System at a 90%+ rate, while leadership teams attempting the journey alone succeed at less than 20%. You'll still gain value working independently, yet trying to facilitate your own organizational transformation is like attempting to perform surgery on yourself. You might understand the theory, but you lack the objectivity, steady hands, outside perspective, and experience necessary for success.

The reason you seek an external resource is the same reason you haven't been able to create breakthroughs on your own. Reading about growth systems won't magically transform your leadership team any more than reading about surgical techniques will turn you into a surgeon.

Uncovering the Invisible Barriers

With trust solidified and limiting beliefs addressed, the second Bloom Quarterly tackles a different challenge: emotional triggers that sabotage team dynamics.

In about 40–50% of our clients, there's a predictable pattern. Someone says something in a certain tone, and another person instantly gets triggered. They take it personally, get defensive, and either respond aggressively or shut down completely. Both responses prevent teams from solving problems effectively. Especially in areas of the business that are already struggling, these reactions make everything worse.

The "Managing Emotional Triggers" exercise helps people actually see what's happening. They can reflect on their reactions, recognize their own part in the dynamic, and imagine a different way of responding. Instead of reacting defensively when someone pushes your buttons, you can choose a different response. You don't have to live in that cycle anymore.

Year 1 takes leaders beyond just managing reactions—it builds something more powerful. Most leadership teams are excellent at resilience, at bouncing back when things go wrong. They're skilled firefighters. What they need is fire prevention. Throughout the year, teams develop robustness: proactive systems and practices that help them navigate challenges with composure rather than constantly recovering from reactions they wish they hadn't made.

The impact ripples through every interaction. Teams that once walked on eggshells now engage in productive debate. Conversations that used to end in frustration become opportunities for deeper understanding. Leaders who spent energy recovering from emotional reactions now channel that energy into strategic thinking and innovation.

By the end of Year 1, what emerges is a leadership team that operates with a new kind of strength. They've moved from constantly putting out fires to preventing them altogether. Difficult conversations become catalysts for growth. Potential conflicts transform into creative problem-solving sessions. The team discovers that when they're not exhausted from managing reactions, they have tremendous energy for building the business they've always envisioned. This is robustness in action—a team that doesn't just survive challenges but uses them as fuel for extraordinary performance.

Ideal Client Identification

Most businesses think they know their best customers. They have hunches and gut feelings about who they should be targeting. When you dig into the actual data, the results are often shocking.

One of our coaches was working with a client convinced their best prospects came through Entrepreneurs' Organization (EO) members. They'd been focusing their networking efforts there, believing those connections led to their most valuable relationships.

The data revealed something surprising: the EO clients were actually their lowest-profit, highest-maintenance accounts. Meanwhile, they had been overlooking Business Network International (BNI) and other peer groups—which turned out to produce their most profitable, lowest-maintenance clients.

This insight only comes from taking a systematic approach. Follow the data, not your feelings.

The Three-Point Analysis

You'll create a comprehensive client analysis with three key data points: lead source, profitability percentage, and total profit generated after factoring in direct and indirect costs. Then you'll start looking for patterns. Once you have the data, insights jump off the page. You might discover that referrals from specific client types are most profitable, or that certain marketing channels consistently produce higher-value customers.

With that data, you'll define your ideal client using one key goal: identify where you can optimize profit with the least effort—the goal is to build a business that scales easier. Revenue size alone doesn't tell the story. A $100,000 client requiring constant hand-holding with 5% margins might be far less valuable than a $50,000 client who runs smoothly with 25% margins.

When you get clear on your ideal client profile, everything becomes more focused. Your marketing becomes laser-targeted. Your sales team knows exactly who to prioritize. You can confidently say no to prospects who don't fit, knowing that energy is better spent attracting clients who will actually drive sustainable growth.

This analysis often reveals that the clients you enjoy working with most are also the most profitable. When there's natural alignment between what you do best and what clients need most, everything flows more smoothly.

Go-to-Market Strategy

Once you're clear on your ideal client, you need a scalable approach to reach them consistently. This means moving beyond random tactics to create a systematic approach that connects your unique value to the right audiences through the right channels.

Your differentiators set you apart from every other option that prospects are considering. The key is identifying ones that are truly scalable—meaning they can be communicated clearly, delivered consistently, and grow with you.

Many businesses compete on price, but this is a race with your competitors to the bottom. Others compete on service or quality, but all companies assert that they have high service and quality. Your differentiators should be defendable, scalable, sustainable and address a pain your ideal clients really want to go away. The strongest differentiators are patents, copyrights, trademarks, established brands, unique suites of services, and scalable relationships. There are more types, but that is not what this book is about—ask AI if you want a full list.

Finding Your Clients Where They Actually Are

Rather than being everything to everyone, effective strategies focus on specific customer segments—distinct groups sharing similar characteristics, challenges, or desired outcomes. These should flow from your ideal client analysis. If manufacturing companies with 50–200 employees are your most profitable clients, that's one bucket. If accounting firm referrals consistently produce high-value relationships, that's another.

Identify two to five specific audience categories where you can focus efforts. This allows targeted messaging, right channel selection, and relationship building where your ideal clients actually spend time.

For growth businesses, the most effective lead generation typically comes from digital platforms and referrals from existing clients as opposed to traditional networking events. While our BNI example earlier shows exceptions exist, most scaling companies find better returns through digital strategies and systematic referral programs. Showing up in AI search results and being recommended by AI platforms is an increasingly critical lead generation channel.

From Strategy to Execution

The most sophisticated strategy means nothing without consistent execution. Your go-to-market strategy should translate into specific weekly KPIs: qualified conversations with prospects in each target segment, outreach to specific segments, content addressing ideal clients' challenges, and networking in the right venues.

The key is connecting weekly activities to quarterly and annual growth goals. When your team knows exactly what to focus on each week, and those activities directly tie to reaching target prospects with scalable and sustainable differentiators, momentum builds naturally.

Sales Process Simplification

One of Isaiah's clients discovered they had 45 distinct steps between initial contact and closing a deal. Forty-five steps. It's no surprise their conversion rates were low and their sales cycles dragged on. Every extra step created another opportunity for prospects to lose interest, get distracted, or stall out.

So they simplified. They cut the unnecessary back-and-forth between departments, eliminated redundant approvals, and streamlined the process from start to finish. The results were dramatic: conversion rates rose, and the sales cycle was cut in half—from 100 days down to 50. What had once been frustrating and drawn out became smooth and efficient for both prospects and the internal team.

This isn't unusual. Most companies find meaningful improvements once they simplify their sales process. The first step is to map it out. Get everything out of your head and onto paper. When leadership teams actually see their process step by step, the complexity is often shocking. What made sense in isolation suddenly looks redundant when viewed as part of the whole.

The goal isn't to eliminate important steps—it's to remove anything that doesn't directly help prospects make a confident buying decision. Every step should either give your team the information they need to serve the client well or help the prospect understand why you're the right solution. Anything else is clutter.

It's also worth paying close attention to handoffs. Every time a prospect is passed from one department to another, risk increases. Friction builds when they have to repeat their story. A wise YPOer once shared that his goal was always to make his business the easiest one in his industry to start a relationship with. That's a powerful standard. Does your process make it easier or harder for qualified prospects to become clients? Each extra hoop creates a barrier to your own success.

When you simplify your sales process, the benefits extend well beyond conversion rates. Your sales team becomes more efficient, prospects enjoy a better experience, and operations are freed up to focus on higher-value work. Most importantly, simple processes scale—complex ones don't.

Process Operational Excellence

Every organization has processes—ways of getting new clients, serving them, and getting paid. These five to seven meaningful processes keep the business running. The problem isn't that processes don't exist; it's that they're often messy, outdated, and not followed.

Consider a $10 million product business with $3 million in payroll. The vast majority of what employees do daily—roughly 80%—consists of recurring tasks they've done before and will do again. That means $2.4 million of payroll goes toward these tasks. Following a systematic approach to optimization can save 20–40% of that time, potentially half a million to a million dollars annually from process improvements alone.

This is strategic work that makes a massive difference.

The Framework for Process Excellence

What really creates impact is identifying the top five to seven most meaningful processes to optimize. Some organizations document hundreds of processes, yet only a handful truly drive the business forward.

Once these top processes are mapped, the next step is measuring speed and quality at multiple points throughout each process. This enables intelligent, continuous improvement conversations. Without measurement, very few organizations become effective at continuously improving their recurring processes.

Each process step needs a clear owner and an agreed-upon timeline. Without clarity on who owns what and when it gets done, teams end up pointing fingers instead of solving problems.

Organizations also need a central repository for processes with version control, permissions for access and updating, and a methodology for continuous improvement. Imagine having 30 salespeople and allowing anyone to change the company's sales process on a whim—it creates chaos that's preventable.

Think of optimized processes as the water on a waterslide. A dry slide means getting stuck, inching along, trying not to get hurt. When the slide is wet, you glide down smoothly with far less effort and much more enjoyment.

When processes flow smoothly, steps get simplified or eliminated entirely. Results happen faster with far less friction, transforming work from stops and starts to freedom and ease.

Servant Leadership vs. Accountability

Here's where we differ from traditional growth models: we focus on servant leadership rather than accountability. Traditional accountability models often rely on fear-based motivation—where performance improvement plans feel more like countdowns than genuine development opportunities.

Our approach takes a fundamentally different path. We believe in creating an environment where accountability emerges naturally through mutual support and helping each other succeed. Leaders learn to genuinely care about their team members as whole people, not just for their business contributions. This means caring about what's best for each person's life and relationships, supporting their growth both professionally and personally.

When you genuinely care about someone and want them to win—not to get something from them, but because you actually care—the entire dynamic shifts. If what's best for someone means pursuing opportunities elsewhere, you become their biggest advocate. Those are the kinds of leaders people want to work with.

Scaling with Human Connection

Supporting all of this growth is our Relationship Curriculum, which has been created to help leaders raise their self-awareness and emotional intelligence. We define emotional intelligence pretty simply: putting yourself in someone else's shoes, seeing the situation from their point of view, and considering that in your communication with them.

Increased self-awareness and genuine caring for the other humans in your life creates the foundation for transformation that doesn't rely on force or coercion, but on authentic human connection and mutual support.

While one of Isaiah's clients quadrupled their net operating income and dramatically increased their operational efficiencies, they said the biggest impact from their Bloom Growth Journey was, "We're better humans because of this." I can't think of a better outcome. When you're flourishing personally, you have the power to get anything you want out of your business.

What to Expect by the End of Year 1

By the end of the year, the leadership team feels energized and empowered. They're moving together as one, driving the business toward its future vision.

This is the kind of transformation that becomes possible when you do the work in Year 1:

- Getting clear on your future
- Building the team that can take you there
- Removing obstacles
- Moving forward—together

It's not just growth. It's sustainable, exciting, energizing growth. The kind that feels good. The kind that makes work fun again.

The opportunity to build a winning team doesn't come around often. When I look back at my career, I can count on one hand the times I've been part of something truly special—where every person was aligned, every strength was maximized, and the collective impact exceeded what anyone thought possible.

Most leaders experience this once, maybe twice in their entire career. The beautiful thing is, it's not luck. It's not timing. It's having the right framework and the commitment to do the work. Working with a Bloom Growth Coach will give you both. The question isn't whether you're capable—you are. The question is simply whether or not this is the moment you choose to build something extraordinary.

We say it all the time:

Let's grow this. Let's go.

Outcomes | Year 1

1. The team becomes aligned around a shared 5-Year Vision with a Growth Plan to get there.
2. Leadership roles are clarified with the right people in the right seats.
3. A rhythm of Bloom Weekly meetings emerges, accelerating sustainable progress at all levels of your organization.
4. Reliable data to predict and forecast the organization's Growth Goals and KPIs.
5. Employees across departments feel more informed, engaged, and aligned, dramatically impacting productivity.

Key Activities | Year 1

- **Attend Seven High-Impact Sessions.** Meet with your Growth Coach for quarterly and annual planning to continuously fine-tune your execution system.
- **Launch Bloom Weekly Meetings Company-Wide.** Expand the powerful weekly cadence from leadership to every level of the organization.
- **Roll Out Quarterly Alignments.** Establish 90-day planning rhythms across all teams to maintain focus and accountability.
- **Refine the 5-Year Vision.** Continuously clarify and communicate the long-term vision to scale with confidence.
- **Map Out Meaningful Processes.** Define ownership and outcomes for key business operations to bring systematic alignment.
- **Integrate Relationship Curriculum.** Embrace Bloom's modern approach to human flourishing to build emotionally intelligent leaders and deeply connected teams.

Bloom Year 2
Scaling with Ease and Compounding the Power of Prioritization

"Listening to others and working together leads to better ideas and more successful outcomes."

— Sir Richard Branson

"To love what you do and feel that it matters—how could anything be more fun?"

— Katharine Graham

When Deep Roots Begin to Bear Fruit

For one of my clients, a $25 million phone call came on a Tuesday morning.

Their most trusted independent sales rep—the one who brought them 70% of their division's business—had been sitting on a major opportunity from Walmart *for years*. He'd mentioned it in passing but never formally made the referral. My client assumed he was working other angles, maybe the timing wasn't right.

They were wrong.

He'd been waiting for them to prove they could handle it.

The breakthrough happened when my client finally addressed a couple operational issues. Their quoting process had been too slow and inconsistent, and sometimes they would miss shipping dates. Once they got those elements dialed in, the sales rep felt confident enough that they could handle the referral.

Here's what actually happened: The independent rep had been watching their operational improvements over several months. He saw their quoting speed and accuracy improve dramatically. He experienced their enhanced on-time delivery firsthand through smaller projects. Most importantly, he witnessed something that's rare in business—a company that was getting progressively better at execution.

The major corporate opportunity had been there all along—he just wasn't confident they could execute at that level. A $25 million project from a Fortune 50 company doesn't offer second chances. One missed deadline, one quality issue, one communication breakdown, and the relationship is over.

As their systems strengthened, so did his confidence. When he finally made the Walmart referral, it wasn't just about a better quoting process—it was about a company that had proven it could identify its weaknesses, fix them systematically, and deliver on its promises.

This is what Year 2 of the Bloom Growth Journey looks like. The foundational work—the leadership team alignment, the weekly rhythms, the disciplined planning—starts to compound. Problems that once seemed overwhelming become visible and solvable. Opportunities that were always there but out of reach suddenly become accessible.

The seeds they planted in Year 1 yielded a Year 2 harvest that exceeded their wildest expectations. The roots you established in Year 1 are now deep enough to support something bigger.

Survey Your Clients and Employees

Year 2 is when we start surveying both clients and employees using simple, three-question surveys that take less than a minute to complete. Having your thumb on the pulse of client and employee happiness allows you to serve both groups better, and these two groups are absolutely vital to every business's successful future.

For employees, we survey quarterly. For clients, we survey every six months, breaking them into six cohorts so we get monthly data without bothering any individual client more than twice a year. When people are willing to give you their time, energy, and money, you treat their feedback like gold and take action on everything.

When Processes Actually Pay Off

You don't start automating processes right when you first map them in Year 1. They need to be iterated on first because they shift and change so much. By Year 2, you're ready for more automation than ever—whether through AI, machinery, or software solutions. The process foundation makes automation actually effective instead of just expensive.

Year 2 is when your process obsession starts paying dividends. Processes become deeply understood and integrated into daily operations. They're continuously being improved, increasing both the speed and quality of everything you do.

Processes become powerful competitive advantages over the first few years as teams measure speed and quality at critical points and commit to continuous improvement. This isn't a six-month project—process perfection is often a 2- to 3-year journey.

Most organizations plateau when they get their processes "good enough" and stop investing energy in continuous improvement. The growing organizations that obsess over process refinement and consistently apply Stop, Automate, Delegate principles over the years are able to build a scalable growth machine.

The difference between good enough and exceptional becomes exponential over time. Small, continuous improvements compound into competitive advantages that competitors struggle to replicate.

The Art of Strategic Quitting

Year 2 introduces one of the most underutilized success principles in business: strategic quitting. While starting the right projects and being tenacious have their place, knowing when and what to stop doing is equally powerful.

The personal energy audit from Day 60 uncovers an uncomfortable pattern. Leaders routinely spend most of their time on activities unrelated to their core priorities. They're stuck handling operational tasks while strategic initiatives sit on the back burner. The real issue runs deeper than poor time management—these leaders haven't built the systems and teams capable of executing independently.

The math is simple but powerful. When you handle work that others could complete at greater than 80% effectiveness, you forfeit time for the strategic initiatives where your unique skills and understanding are essential. Building the confidence to delegate operational tasks opens the door to genuine strategic leadership.

This is where continuous improvement accelerates. As teams master the discipline of strategic quitting and process refinement, they create capacity for innovation, strategic thinking, and the kind of leadership presence that transforms organizations.

Simplifying and Optimizing Technology

Most businesses treat technology like a toolbox, constantly adding new tools without organizing what's already inside. This creates a chaotic collection of platforms that generate more work instead of less.

Your current tech stack probably has untapped potential hiding in plain sight. When you conduct a comprehensive audit of all your software platforms, you'll likely make a surprising discovery: your company has accumulated multiple tools that overlap significantly, while valuable features in your existing platforms sit unused.

This audit reveals two types of opportunities. First, you'll identify redundant subscriptions. Most teams find 10–20% waste from duplicate software across departments. Second, you'll uncover powerful features you're already paying for but not using, eliminating the need for additional tools.

The transformation happens when you approach technology strategically on two fronts: streamlining internal operations and enhancing client experience. Internally, you're consolidating platforms and training teams to maximize existing capabilities. Externally, you're removing friction from every client touchpoint.

One of my clients, a commercial and industrial roofing contractor, exemplifies this approach. They eliminated their outdated 3-part carbon copy forms and clipboards, replacing them with iPads that generate quotes and book business instantly. What previously required a week-long "we'll get back to you" process became immediate email confirmation on-site. This single change dramatically improved their closing rates by eliminating the gap where prospects could change their minds or find competitors.

The transformation extends beyond operational improvements to cultural change. When your team has streamlined tools that actually work together, decision-making accelerates. When clients experience seamless interactions at every touchpoint, trust builds faster. Your technology stack becomes a competitive advantage, positioning your company as both efficient and forward-thinking.

Focus on Finance and Data

You can't manage what you don't measure. Financial clarity means knowing your numbers inside and out—your revenue, margins, cash flow, and KPIs that really matter—so you can make smart decisions quickly and confidently.

In Year 2, we introduce the Cash Optimization Tool for Finance and Data—your guide to understanding which financial moves actually make a difference in your cash flow and profits. The power of this tool lies in its precision. A 1% improvement in the right area can dramatically impact your bottom line, and those small changes add up over time into significant financial gains.

You'll work with a clear spending plan (most people call this a budget) that shows you the direct connection between your decisions and cash flow outcomes. Instead of guessing which changes will help your business, you'll learn to spot the specific levers that create the most meaningful impact on your organization's financial health.

Monthly P&L meetings keep you on track by letting you review progress against your spending plan and cash flow targets while giving you the chance to course-correct quickly when needed.

By focusing on profit optimization—increasing margins and maximizing return on effort—you'll replace leadership anxiety with confidence. Understanding your numbers means you can guide your business with vision rather than reaction, creating a financial management system that drives sustainable growth, year after year.

The Sales and Marketing Machine Hits Its Stride

The sales and marketing system hits its stride in Year 2. You got clear on your ideal client and go-to-market strategy in Year 1. Now you have the right people in the right seats, processes in place, and the right software—usually a CRM—all aligned around your sales and marketing ecosystem. It starts to flourish, and beyond that, it becomes scalable.

Before, selling might have depended on one or two uniquely awesome salespeople. Now it's process-driven and repeatable. Trust increases dramatically as you serve clients with improved processes, speed, and communication. Often in Year 2, referrals from existing clients and customers become one of your top two lead sources.

Your existing client retention and growth goes up too, and these things are completely related. More referrals, better retention, clients spending more with you—it all stems from becoming a better business, both in how you're structured as well as how you align people and processes around serving clients.

Inclusion, Feedback, and Flow

What makes Year 2 so powerful isn't just that things are running smoothly—it's that more people than ever feel *part of it.*

As Bloom Growth expands across the organization, the system begins to reach every corner of the business. The employees often left out of the decision-making process are now brought into the communication rhythm through quarterly alignments with their managers.

Meanwhile, the Relationship dimension deepens. In Year 2, leaders are trained not just to lead—but to *manage* with purpose. They develop skills in giving and receiving feedback, coaching for performance, and aligning team values through everyday conversations. This level of emotional intelligence and clarity doesn't just improve outcomes—it strengthens relationships. Leadership becomes less about control and more about connection. And it shows.

By now, the feedback loop is humming. Client and employee surveys are built into the quarterly and biannual rhythms, and every person is part of the business getting better.

Empowerment at Every Level

As the leadership team elevates and becomes more strategic, distilling tactical issues down to where they belong, a transformation takes root—people throughout the organization become genuinely empowered and engaged.

By Year 2, the entire organization operates in sync. All departments maintain weekly team rhythms, every employee participates in quarterly alignment sessions with their manager, and the system serves as a company-wide communication platform.

Everyone gets involved in co-creating the business. When you're helping to make decisions that matter, you naturally want to see them succeed. It's similar to involving children when planting a garden. They're much more likely to eat the vegetables that they helped to plant.

The momentum that builds as you roll this out organization-wide is incredible. The amount of clarity that comes company-wide is unlike anything most businesses have ever experienced.

Outcomes | Year 2

1. Everyone understands the vision and their role in achieving it with organization-wide clarity and engagement.
2. Your second year's goals are leading you progressively closer to your organization's 3-Year Future and 5-Year Vision.
3. Increased client satisfaction combined with strong processes fuel predictable revenue and increased referrals.
4. Trusted partners, clients, and team members recognize your capacity to deliver at a higher level, creating opportunities that flow more easily.

5. Systems become refined and reliable, delivering operational excellence that increases speed, quality, and trust.
6. Leaders coach and empower others, creating contagious leadership that multiplies impact across teams.

Key Activities | Year 2

- **Diagnose and Resolve Key Bottlenecks.** Identify and eliminate high-leverage operational constraints that are holding back growth.
- **Lock in Process Maturity and Automation.** Iterate key processes until stable, then implement the right tools to automate workflows.
- **Activate the Sales & Marketing Engine.** Build repeatable, process-driven growth systems with CRM integration and continuous feedback loops.
- **Solidify Leadership Structure.** Refine the top two organizational layers with the right people in the right seats owning clear outcomes.
- **Develop Department Leaders.** Train department heads to give effective feedback, coach performance, and embed company values daily.

From 76% to 96% Shipping Accuracy— The Power of Process Mapping

After scaling six companies using growth operating systems, **Kim Latko** now helps other entrepreneurs achieve breakthrough results as a Bloom Growth Coach.

My first company started with an accidental invention that went viral during the Beanie Baby phenomenon. When the fad crashed, I had two options: close the doors or completely reinvent the business.

Working with a growth operating system gave me the framework to transform that single-product idea into a sustainable manufacturing operation. Since then, I've scaled six companies and experienced firsthand how having both a proven system and a coach makes the difference between surviving and thriving.

Today, I rely on Bloom Growth to scale my global event-supply business through the complexities of international sourcing, licensing, and rapid expansion. The system has been my compass through both boom times and crises. During economic downturns, it kept my teams focused on the right metrics and maintained momentum when markets stalled.

The tool that consistently delivers breakthrough results is process mapping. Recently, I worked with a client whose shipping accuracy was stuck at 76%. Their process was unclear, inconsistent, and riddled with bottlenecks. Using Bloom Growth's process mapping framework, we documented every step, identified where things broke down, and streamlined each stage.

The transformation was immediate. Accuracy began climbing the very next week. Today, they track their KPIs daily in the Bloom software, average 96% accuracy, and are steadily approaching their goal of 100%. Process mapping turned their biggest weakness into a competitive advantage.

I coach because I'm endlessly curious about finding patterns and uncovering opportunities. Having lived the growth journey through wins, pivots, and tough seasons, I now walk alongside other entrepreneurs as they scale with confidence, clarity, and purpose.

Kim Latko,
Entrepreneur & Bloom Growth Coach, North America

Get Connected

To have an experienced Bloom Growth Coach—an entrepreneur who's actually scaled companies—speak to your leadership team about your company's untapped potential, scan the QR code below or reach out to the coach who shared this book with you.

Jeremy Giroir
Bloom Growth Coach

+1 337.298.8323

bloomgrowthcoach.com/get-connected

——————————————— Bloom
Year 3 and Beyond
Getting What You Want

"What you do makes a difference,
and you have to decide what kind of
difference you want to make."
——————————————————— Jane Goodall

"The quality of our relationships
determines the quality of our lives."
——————————————— Julie Schwartz Gottman, PhD

The Journey of Growth and Transformation

At the beginning of this journey, we promised to help you get what you want from your business. For many, that's predictable and sustainable growth, time freedom, and improved relationships. By Year 3 and beyond, you're positioned to achieve all of the above.

Remember, the path to achieving your 5-Year Vision begins with building your ideal leadership team in Year 1 and aligning the entire organization with the right people in the right seats to increase the speed and quality of every recurring process by the end of Year 2.

As you enter Year 3, the transformation of the culture deepens so that employees, clients, and vendors experience human flourishing. Year 4 is all about exceeding your wildest expectations in financial performance and impact, and by Year 5, you get to celebrate achieving your organization's 5-Year Vision.

For a visual progression, see the graphic on the next page:

The Path to Achieving Your 5-Year Vision

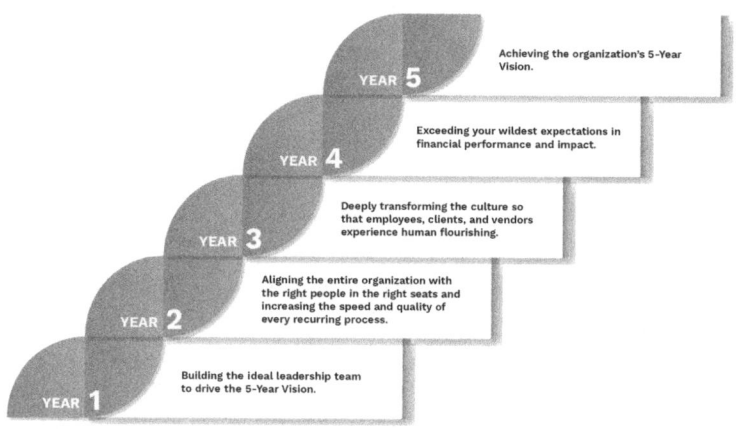

YEAR 5 — Achieving the organization's 5-Year Vision.

YEAR 4 — Exceeding your wildest expectations in financial performance and impact.

YEAR 3 — Deeply transforming the culture so that employees, clients, and vendors experience human flourishing.

YEAR 2 — Aligning the entire organization with the right people in the right seats and increasing the speed and quality of every recurring process.

YEAR 1 — Building the ideal leadership team to drive the 5-Year Vision.

Sustained Momentum, Lasting Legacy

When a business follows a structured path to growth, everything changes for the better. Conversations shift from reactionary to forward-focused. Leaders begin to see a clear vision for where they're going, moving from simply surviving the day to actively driving the future. The stress of uncertainty fades, replaced by a shared sense of purpose and a collective drive to succeed.

While the first 90 days of launching the Growth OS are crucial, it's only the beginning. As you move into the next phases—quarterly, yearly, and beyond—pent-up potential blooms.

Over the span of two to four years, the organization refines, expands, and simplifies its operations, building a rhythm that gets better with time.

What you can expect:

- The top two layers of the Ideal Leadership Team Structure take between 9 and 24 months to perfect; when those layers align, everything clicks.
- The relationships among team members become stronger than ever.
- The clarity and unity felt within the team fuels not just the business but also personal growth and connection.
- The relationships are next-level, and for many, they're the best they've ever had in their personal and professional lives.

The real excitement comes after two to three years of refining and expanding the business. At this point, the company isn't just growing—it's operating as a thriving system.

This is where things get really thrilling. At this point, the business has become a dynamic, growing force that runs with precision yet adapts with ease. Leaders and teams move with confidence, fueled by a shared vision and a deep sense of ownership.

Growth is no longer a grind; it's an ongoing evolution that energizes everyone involved. And with each step forward, the business becomes more than a company—it becomes a legacy.

From One Restaurant to 13 Locations— Preserving a Multi-Generational Legacy

Anish Patel transformed from entrepreneur to Growth Coach after experiencing firsthand how growth systems can save businesses—and built a practice spanning India, Sri Lanka, and Nepal.

I had two very young entrepreneurs in Sri Lanka who acquired the business from their uncle. It was the oldest restaurant in the heart of Colombo. They wanted to preserve the family legacy and expand the brand.

When they first came to me, they had a goal and a vision to make it into a chain of food outlets. Not just growth from increasing revenue in the same restaurant. They wanted multiple locations and multiple revenue streams across Sri Lanka.

The pressure was immense. Whether you inherit or acquire a family business, the entire family is watching. Every uncle, aunt, cousin, and grandparent has an opinion. There's no room for mistakes when you're operating in that spotlight—the family legacy is at stake, and everyone cares about it for their own reasons.

These young men weren't just trying to pay bills. They were carrying the weight of generations on their shoulders, knowing that failure would mean letting down not just themselves, but their entire extended family. That kind of pressure can paralyze decision-making.

But with Bloom Growth OS, they found a proven system that dramatically increased their odds of success. By Year 3 of their Bloom Growth Journey, they had 13 outlets. They had added a catering business as their second revenue stream. Then they launched a high-end confectionery business for celebrations.

What started as two young entrepreneurs trying to honor their uncle's legacy became something far greater—13 locations, three revenue streams, and a business that exceeded every family member's expectations.

The transformation was so powerful that one of the brothers now serves as a Bloom Growth Coach himself, helping other businesses across South Asia navigate the growth journey.

Anish Patel,
Bloom Growth Coach, India Community Leader

———————Epic Event
The Ideal Exit Strategy for Business Owners and Team Leaders

"The best time to prepare for your exit is the day you start your business. The second-best time is today."

——————————————— Byron McFarland

"You didn't come this far to only come this far."

——————————————— Jamie Kern Lima

The Freedom Most People Wait a Lifetime For

There's a reason people crave retirement: it's traditionally the first time in their lives when they concurrently have freedom of time and money. You can have freedom of time as a college student or when unemployed, but you're broke. You can have freedom of money by working intensely, but you sacrifice your time. Retirement represents that sweet spot where both freedoms converge—usually sometime in your 60s.

Here's what makes entrepreneurship so appealing: you don't have to wait until retirement. Through building and systematically growing your business, you can achieve freedom of time and money in your 30s, 40s, or 50s. It's phenomenal, and it's available to you now.

Making It Comfortable to Discuss

Most business sales happen in secrecy, with employees learning about the transaction only after it's complete. This approach breeds fear and resentment because employees aren't engaged in maximizing the business value or invited to be stakeholders in the outcome.

The respectful approach is transparency. When everyone understands what's in it for them—clear, positive outcomes that are exciting for both owners and team members—the conversation becomes collaborative rather than threatening. Both parties win, and everyone can work together toward the shared vision of success.

A Note to Owners

By Year 3, you have real choices. You might choose to exit your business entirely through an Epic Event (this section is for you). Or you might prefer to step back from day-to-day operations while maintaining ownership, allowing your professionally managed leadership team to run the business while you focus on the things you love and do best.

Either path represents true freedom—the kind where you spend as much or as little time as you want in the business, doing work that energizes you rather than drains you.

A Note to the Leadership Team

This journey isn't just about the owner's freedom—it's about creating opportunities for everyone involved. As the business grows systematically, leadership team members experience greater responsibility, increased compensation, and expanded opportunities for their future.

When an exit does occur, there are typically financial incentives in place for leaders and often all employees. You're not just building someone else's dream—you're building shared success where everyone benefits from the value created together.

The Ultimate Business Transition

Your Epic Event might feel both exciting and terrifying. This is the moment when you transition out of the business you've poured your heart, soul, and countless late nights into. Whether that means selling to a strategic buyer, passing it on to family, or handing the reins to your leadership team, your Epic Event represents the culmination of everything you've built.

Most business owners approach this backwards, though. They wait until they're ready to leave before they start thinking about what that actually looks like. It's like deciding to run a marathon and only starting to train the week before the race. Sure, you might cross the finish line, but it's going to be painful, and you're probably not going to achieve the results you dreamed of.

The Reality Check

Let me share a sobering statistic with you: 80% of businesses that go to market never actually sell. Not because they're bad businesses, but because they weren't prepared for what buyers are actually looking for. Think about that for a moment—four out of five business owners who decide they're ready for their Epic Event walk away empty-handed, often after months (or years) of stress, disruption, and disappointment.

The businesses that do successfully transition? They didn't just get lucky. They understood something crucial: preparation isn't a six-month sprint before you want to exit. It's a strategic mindset that shapes how you build and run your business from day one.

What Buyers Really Want

When potential buyers evaluate your business—whether private equity firms, strategic acquirers, or your own management team—they look beyond your products or services. They're assessing whether your systems, culture, and operations can deliver consistent results without you at the helm.

This reality might feel uncomfortable, but it's actually your biggest opportunity. Buyers pay premium prices for businesses that run independently of their founders. By building something so solid, so well-organized, and so strategically positioned that it thrives without your daily involvement, you create exactly what sophisticated buyers want: a predictable, profitable business that doesn't require them to step into your shoes.

Buyers are looking for businesses that are:

- **Financially transparent**: Your books are clean, your metrics are clear, and your financial story makes sense.
- **Operationally excellent**: Your processes don't live in your head—they're documented, repeatable, and scalable.
- **Leadership-ready**: You have a strong team that can execute without you.
- **Market-positioned**: You have a clear competitive advantage—with defendable, scalable differentiators—and a proven growth machine that will continue to grow post-transaction.

The Secret Weapon

Many business owners get this wrong by thinking Epic Event preparation is a solo mission—something they need to figure out behind closed doors before involving anyone else. Through working with thousands of businesses all over the world, we've discovered that doing things secretly or in silos actually undermines the intended outcome. The truth is, your leadership team is your secret weapon.

When you involve your senior leaders in Epic Event preparation, several powerful things happen:

First, you get their insights into what makes your business truly valuable. They see opportunities and strengths that you might take for granted. Second, their engagement in the process makes them stronger leaders, which directly impacts your business value. And third, buyers want to see a leadership team that's invested, informed, and ready to drive the business forward.

Think about it from a buyer's perspective: Would you rather acquire a business where the owner is the linchpin, or one where there's a capable, engaged leadership team that clearly understands the vision and strategy?

The workshop approach changes everything for business owners who want to prepare strategically. Rather than trying to figure everything out alone, you get your entire leadership team aligned on what your Epic Event could look like and what it will take to get there.

The most successful business owners we work with begin with a focused, intensive workshop that brings their senior team together to:

- Understand what buyers are really evaluating when they look at businesses like yours
- Identify the gaps between where you are now and where you need to be
- Create a clear action plan that strengthens your business while positioning it for a successful transition
- Align the entire leadership team on the vision and the shared financial incentives for making it happen

Rather than creating more work for your already busy team, you're channeling the work you're already doing toward building a more valuable, more transferable business.

The Benefits Start Immediately

The beautiful part about preparing for your Epic Event properly is that the work you do to make your business more attractive to buyers makes it more profitable and less dependent on you right now. Better systems, stronger leadership, clearer financials, and strategic positioning don't just help with a future sale—they improve today's operations.

Business owners who think strategically about their Epic Event often find that:

- Their businesses become more profitable as systems improve

- They have more freedom as their leadership teams grow and become more robust
- They sleep better at night knowing their business isn't entirely dependent on them
- They have more strategic options when the time comes to transition

Getting ready to sell a business is kind of like getting ready to sell a house—once you make all the changes your buyer would expect, you find that it's exactly what you want and might decide to stay. We see that happen often, and when it does, the entire business gets infused with a fresh level of energy and excitement.

Morale improves, productivity soars, and everyone breathes a collective sigh, knowing that for now, they don't have to prepare for big changes, but when the time comes, they're ready.

Your Epic Event, Your Timeline

The goal isn't to push you toward an exit before you're ready. It's to ensure that when you are ready—whether that's in two years or twenty—you have options. Exciting options. And you get to choose the path that aligns with your values, your financial goals, and your vision for the business you've built.

Your Epic Event should be epic not just because of the financial outcome, but because it represents the successful completion of what you set out to build: a business that creates value for customers, opportunities for employees, and legacy for you.

The question isn't whether you'll eventually have an Epic Event. The question is whether you'll be prepared when that moment comes.

When you're ready to start preparing for your Epic Event, your Bloom Growth Coach can help you eliminate blind spots and avoid pitfalls. The journey begins with understanding where you are today and what it will take to get you where you want to go. Your future self—and your business—will thank you for starting now.

——— An Invitation
Transform Other Businesses While Growing Your Own Impact

Are you a successful entrepreneur who's navigated the challenges of scaling a business and now wants to help others avoid the same pitfalls? Are you in transition between ventures or looking toward your next chapter with a desire to make a meaningful difference?

Built by entrepreneurs, for entrepreneurs, the Bloom Growth Coach Community represents an elite group of business leaders who've chosen to multiply their impact by guiding other leadership teams through proven growth frameworks.

As a Bloom Growth Coach, you'll work alongside fellow entrepreneurs who share your passion for building healthy, thriving businesses. You'll guide leadership teams through the same structured journey outlined in this book—from Day 1 foundation-setting through years of sustained growth—using the 8 Essentials and proven methodologies you've just learned.

Our Coach Community Core Values

Before you consider joining us, take an honest look at these core values. If your closest relationships wouldn't describe you as naturally embodying these qualities, please don't reach out. We're looking for coaches who live these values authentically:

Have a Great Attitude

- **Helpful**: Actively support clients, peers, and Bloom Growth
- **Humble**: Stay grounded in interactions and online presence; clients are always the hero of their success stories, never the coach
- **Kind**: Treat others as they want to be treated, both to their face and behind their back
- **Positive**: Foster an uplifting environment; share constructive feedback directly with Bloom Growth leadership
- **Grateful**: Recognize that this work is a privilege and live from a place of appreciation
- **Loving**: Care genuinely for yourself, peers, and clients in workplace-appropriate ways

Grow Daily

- Commit to continuous personal improvement mentally, physically, and emotionally
- Embrace being a lifelong learner with curiosity over know-it-all attitudes
- Collaborate within our community and compete in the marketplace—never compete with fellow coaches

Do the Right Thing

- Make great choices based on our core values
- Take responsibility and seek permanent solutions without blaming others or circumstances

- Honor your word by keeping promises to yourself, peers, and clients

Abundance Mentality/Give First

- Help others without expectation of return
- Recognize that through unconditional giving, everyone grows—you, your clients, and our community
- Understand that giving often enriches your own life, directly or indirectly

Ready to Learn More?

If these values resonate deeply with who you are and how you operate, we'd love to explore whether you're a fit for our coaching community.

Learn more about becoming a Bloom Growth Coach:

bloomgrowth.com/coach

Scan me

Join a community where your entrepreneurial experience becomes the foundation for transforming other businesses—and where your next chapter becomes your most meaningful one yet.

──────────To Sum Up

"Wealth is merely useful for the sake of something else."

── Aristotle

"Human well-being or flourishing ... consists in a much broader range of states and outcomes, certainly including mental and physical health, but also encompassing happiness and life satisfaction, meaning and purpose, character and virtue, and close social relationships."

── Tyler J. VanderWeele,
The Human Flourishing Program, Harvard University

TL;DR Summary

If you're anything like me, you appreciate a quick 5-page summary of books instead of taking the time to read them from cover to cover. This section is just that—I'm not going to tell you to go back and read the book from the beginning. I'm just going to summarize key concepts because people like me always skip to the end.

In a nutshell, if your business is either growing so fast that your internal systems and people can't keep up, or you're experiencing stalled growth and need help getting out of the rut, you're in the right place. Either way, the Bloom Growth Operating System (BGOS) is the key to get things moving in a direction where everyone wins.

What Makes Bloom Growth Different

Here's what sets Bloom Growth OS apart: It's not only about building a better business by giving teams the tools, structures, priorities, and frameworks they need to gain control and grow but also about human flourishing—building stronger bonds and taking relationships to the next level.

Most growth systems focus exclusively on processes, metrics, and execution. They treat people like resources to be optimized rather than humans to be developed. Bloom Growth OS recognizes that sustainable growth happens when both the business and the people inside it are thriving.

A Growth OS is primarily for two types of organizations:

1. Businesses that are finding it hard to keep up with the rate at which they're growing. They've often mastered sales and marketing but need support in structuring their teams and systems to support that growth in a more robust and scalable way.
2. Businesses that want to grow faster and in a more sustainable and predictable way. They're ready and eager to scale into a next-level future, but haven't figured out how to grow revenue and profit at the rate they want.

The methods described in this book will help you get more of what you want out of your business (growth, freedom, and fun) and less of what you don't want (struggle, grind, and frustration). But growth isn't a one-time event. It's a series of intentional steps, each one building on the last.

The journey starts with open, honest, vulnerable, transparent, and authentic communication. If your leadership team is unwilling to have difficult conversations or follow a proven system, Bloom Growth won't do you any good.

If you're not satisfied with "good enough," can't stand the thought of "just getting by," and you're willing to put in the effort toward growth, this system will take you to the heights you've always imagined.

The Growth Multiplier Effect

As the organization grows, the people working there experience something powerful: they get new and more interesting opportunities, and they get paid more. They experience personal, professional, and financial growth as the business grows. This isn't just a nice side effect—it's the fundamental driver of sustained momentum.

When employees get to be part of building the business, they take genuine pride in it. They're contributing to something bigger than themselves, and their work becomes more meaningful because they can see their direct impact on the company's success.

If you're with a business that's growing, there's more opportunity for promotion, more interesting projects, and more financial rewards. People in entrepreneurial growth firms are usually wired this way already—they're motivated by the chance to grow alongside the organization.

But if you have people inside your growth organization who don't believe in this alignment, who aren't motivated by personal, professional, and financial growth, they shouldn't be there. Growth organizations need people who understand that everybody wins when the organization wins.

Transformation from the Inside Out

When we talk about launching Bloom Growth OS, what happens in the first 90 days is genuinely transformative. This is where the momentum begins, the groundwork is laid, and the culture starts to shift. Here's what you can expect across the entire system:

Business Foundation: Your leadership team will establish clear priorities, communication rhythms, and accountability structures. You'll identify and begin addressing the key issues that have been holding your growth back. Decision-making becomes faster and more aligned as everyone operates from the same playbook.

Human Development: Leaders begin doing the inner work needed to unlock growth, transform their personal and professional relationships, and lead with purpose, authenticity, and confidence. We create psychological safety and trust, so that team leaders feel able to share their beliefs, stories, and leadership styles without fear of being attacked or looked down on by others.

Cultural Transformation: We challenge assumptions and begin uncovering the limiting beliefs and internal stories that hold teams back, helping leaders become more self-aware of the patterns driving suboptimal outcomes. At the same time, we build emotional connection and deep team rapport, so team leaders can get beyond surface knowledge of each other and start to create deeper bonds, which are critical for performance.

Systems Integration: The tools, frameworks, and processes begin working together as a cohesive operating system rather than disconnected initiatives. Your team starts to experience the power of alignment (when everyone is rowing in the same direction with clarity and purpose). The Bloom Growth software is also an intuitive solution for alignment across execution, communication, and meetings.

As each individual member of the leadership team becomes fluent in self-awareness and self-regulation (emotional mastery), their relational and influence skills improve. The quality and depth of conversation centers around these capabilities, which build on each other and lead to human flourishing.

But let's be clear—Day 1 to Day 90 is not the finish line. It's not even close. It's the beginning.

Beyond the Launch

In the grand scheme of the Bloom Journey, this launch phase represents only about 5% of the entire transformation. It's the spark, not the fire. What lies ahead is the real journey: one that refines, expands, and simplifies your systems quarter after quarter, year after year.

From Day 90 onward, everything gets more powerful.

As you move through quarterly sessions and annual retreats over the next two, three, even four years, the Growth OS becomes a way of life. It doesn't just change how the business runs—it changes how people lead, how they connect, and how they grow.

During Year 1, organizations are getting the right people in the right seats in their departments. They're building their dream team for the next level. At the same time, they're identifying where they're stuck—whether through process breakdowns, leadership gaps, technology needs, or operational constraints.

As these stuck points get resolved, organizations experience cascading breakthroughs. Maybe it's finally building out a sales team that's scalable, streamlining quoting and pricing, and dramatically improving response times and conversion rates. Maybe it's identifying that growth will come through acquisitions and building KPIs around that strategy.

Energy builds as teams take ownership of their business components. Leadership team members aren't overwhelmed anymore because they have entire departments aligned and helping them.

When you clarify what needs to be addressed—whether it's a growth strategy, operational processes, or team development—and you align the pieces with the right communication rhythms, transformation accelerates. You can engage the entire system and begin scaling with confidence.

As you build out the top layers of your Ideal Leadership Team Structure (a process that takes anywhere from 9 to 24 months), communication is mastered. Organizational energy becomes focused and contagious. You begin to experience the rare alchemy created by a team that loves playing the game and gets better at it every time they come together.

This is when personal and professional relationships hit their highest levels.

People describe it as the most aligned, most creative, and most deeply satisfying season of their lives. Business metrics improve, sure, but what matters even more is that trust deepens, conversations elevate, and energy flows.

And then—around years three or four—something incredible happens.

You've refined your systems. You've simplified complexity. You've scaled with clarity. And now? You're ready to unlock a whole new level of the game.

This is where the journey goes from inspiring to electric.

The Epic Event

The business is humming along with more ease and predictability than anyone ever dreamed possible. At this point, some owners decide to stay and enjoy the ride while others seek the payoff they've been working toward for years (some of them for their entire adult lives).

The Epic Event is designed not just to celebrate success, but to share it. To create generational opportunity, to reward the entire team, and to make decisions not from urgency, but from abundance.

The Epic Event is not the end. It's the reward for doing the work well, over time, with heart, integrity, and joy.

And everyone wins.

BONUS: 15 Simple, Proven Ways to Unleash Pent-Up Business Potential

It's common for businesses to start strong, growing beautifully, only to plateau or hit an obstacle. Even if some areas of your business are thriving, there's a good chance others might be creating a bottleneck.

From our experience working with fast-growing companies, we've identified 15 specific areas that, when addressed, consistently release massive growth. The good news is that you don't have to pull all 15 levers. You can focus on just the top one to three to get you moving in the right direction.

The Method

Gather your leadership team and go through each principle (while there are 15 listed, you'll notice some overlap), and explain the concept briefly to your team. Then have each team member individually rate how well you are doing as an organization in each of the 15 areas.

To get the most out of this activity, have each leader individually rate your company on a scale of 1 to 3. The scale is as follows:

| **1:** We have a lot of work to do. | **2:** We're okay but could improve. | **3:** We're excelling in this area. |

You might be tempted to collaborate with each other, but it's essential that each team member keeps the ratings private until the very end. I can't emphasize this enough.

Do not collaborate with your team during this exercise!

Once everyone has rated each principle, we'll combine the scores to identify the top three actionable areas for improvement. By pulling one to three of these levers and making an inspiring permanent change in the way that your business operates, you'll unlock pent-up energy to create new momentum.

1. Right People, Right Seats

The first principle is ensuring your leadership team has the **right people in the right seats.** This is critical for taking your organization to the next level.

Next, consider the teams reporting to your leadership—your department teams. These first two layers of the organization (leadership and direct reports) are essential for growth.

- **Right People:** These are individuals who align with your culture. Think of it as a "no jerks" policy—people who are enjoyable to work with and share your organization's values.
- **Right Seats:** Roles and responsibilities required to move the business forward that align with each person's natural skills and strengths—things they want to do, are great at, and they're succeeding.

Rate your leadership team and their direct reports on how close they are to being the right people in the right seats:

| **1:** We have a lot of work to do. | **2:** We're okay but could improve. | **3:** We're excelling in this area. |

2. Attracting and Retaining Talent

Does your organization have a strong system for **identifying, attracting, recruiting, and onboarding** talent? This ensures you're never left with open roles hindering growth.

Rate how effective your recruiting and retention processes are:

| **1:** Processes are ineffective and require significant leadership involvement. | **2:** Systems are inconsistent; sometimes they work, sometimes they don't. | **3:** Recruiting and retention are seamless, well-oiled functions |

3. KPIs—Predictive and Measurable Metrics

Key Performance Indicators (KPIs) are the **weekly activities** that predict and produce desired outcomes. These metrics should link to your growth goals and allow you to track progress effectively.

Rate your organization:

| **1:** Poor at tracking predictive activities. Outcomes are often a surprise. | **2:** Partially effective but not a consistent system. | **3:** KPIs are clear, predictive, and consistently guide our decisions and we're achieving our growth goals. |

4. Process—Speed and Quality of Recurring Tasks

Processes are about improving the speed and quality of recurring tasks, which typically account for 80–90% of payroll dollars. Streamlining processes can yield massive efficiency gains.

Rate your processes:

1: Processes are disorganized or nonexistent.	**2:** Some documentation and training are in place but need improvement.	**3:** Processes are efficient, measurable, continuously improving, and used consistently.

5. Finance—Spending Plan (Budget)

Consider your financial planning. Whether you call it a budget or a spending plan (my personal favorite), the goal is to ensure your organization has a proactive plan for how money flows to support growth.

Rate your finance function:

1: Poor understanding or lack of a clear plan.	**2:** Some financial planning, but it's inconsistent, reactive, and often only involves ownership	**3:** Finance is a well-managed, forward-looking function and our leadership team is referencing our financial reality for decision making all the time.

6. Scalable Sales and Marketing

You need systems in place to grow faster, easier, and more cost-effectively. Is your sales and marketing strategy scalable, efficient, and winning?

Rate your organization:

1: Significant room for improvement.	**2:** Decent but inconsistent results.	**3:** Sales and marketing are optimized for growth and winning.

7. Retention and Growth of Existing Clients

As a Growth Coach, I've found the real gold often lies in **retaining and growing existing clients**, not just acquiring new ones. Most leadership teams have a sales and marketing leader focused on new business, but the most successful teams also prioritize retention. Some even have a dedicated leader for this area. When we analyze the ROI, the results are phenomenal. Departments that actively focus on retaining and growing existing clients consistently outperform expectations.

How does your organization handle retention and growth of existing clients? Is it an afterthought, or does it get real attention?

Rate your organization:

1: There is a significant gap.	**2:** We're doing okay, but could improve.	**3:** Retention and growth are core strengths of our business.

8. Decisive People Moves

In my years of coaching leadership teams, I've seen that **half of their challenges stem from avoiding difficult people decisions**. Whether it's reassigning roles, hiring, or letting someone go, decisive people moves unlocks growth.

This isn't just about firing. Often, it's about **realigning roles** to fit people's strengths. For example, "Sally" excels at half her job but struggles with the other half. How quickly does your organization recognize this and reassign her responsibilities? Making this move benefits both the company and Sally—she gets to shine, and the organization becomes more efficient.

Sometimes it means **hiring strategically**. If you need eight salespeople but only have six, how quickly can you secure the budget and onboard the right talent? Other times, it involves addressing tough conversations, especially if the wrong person is in a role they can't succeed in. Delaying those conversations doesn't help anyone—it hinders the organization and stalls their career.

Even when personal relationships complicate matters, avoiding the right decision is no excuse.

How decisive are you regarding people moves?

1: This is a major area of weakness.	**2**: It's a work in progress.	**3**: Our team is highly effective at making tough and timely people decisions.

9. Culture—Growing Together

All of our fastest-growing clients share one thing in common: **a commitment to culture**. They obsess and invest in it through good times and bad. Our mantra is simple: **"Have fun growing together."**

How much do you obsess and invest in your culture?

| **1**: Culture is not a priority. | **2**: We're making some effort but could do more. | **3**: Culture is thriving, even during challenges. |

10. Growing Your People

To sustain growth and lead your industry, you must prioritize **training and development**. Whether you call it a company university, professional development, or something else, what matters is your commitment to ongoing learning.

This goes beyond onboarding. Continuous training builds a team aligned with your culture, reduces turnover, and saves money in the long run. High turnover and constant recruiting are far more expensive than investing in your people.

Rate your training and development program:

| **1**: It's inadequate or nonexistent. | **2**: We're doing some training, but it's not enough. | **3**: Training and development are core strengths. |

11. Celebrating Growth

Does your organization celebrate growth, or do you have a **"sales prevention department"**? This refers to teams—often in operations or finance—that resent new sales because it creates more work for them.

Growth should always be celebrated, not resented. Whether it's ringing a bell for a big win or recognizing the team's hard work, celebrating creates momentum. If your organization discourages growth, it's time to shift the mindset.

Rate your celebration of growth:

| **1**: Growth is met with resistance or negativity. | **2**: It's occasionally celebrated, but not consistently. | **3**: Growth is embraced and regularly celebrated. |

12. Customer and Employee Feedback

Accurate, relevant, and timely feedback is essential for growth. Relying on gut instinct isn't enough—having systems in place to gather meaningful customer and employee feedback is critical. The best organizations use this data to make informed decisions and drive improvement.

Do you regularly collect and act on feedback?

| **1**: Feedback systems are inadequate or nonexistent. | **2**: You're doing a little, but there's room for improvement. | **3**: Feedback is timely, actionable, and a key part of your strategy. |

13. Planning Process

Having a regular cadence for aligning all the energy in your organization around pivotal priorities is critical. There are many planning methodologies out there, and one of the roles of a Growth Coach is to help you find the one that works best for you.

Here's the challenge: left to our own devices, we tend to prioritize what's interesting, urgent, or easy. But those are the enemies of a solid planning process. Instead, your north star must always be the most important priorities—the ones that will help you double your business and achieve your short- and long-term goals.

How well is your planning process serving you?

1: We don't have a planning process—we're just winging it.	2: We have a methodology, but it's not being used effectively.	3: Our planning process is a well-oiled machine.

14. Growth Capital

Depending on your business model, growth capital—whether debt or equity—might be a necessity to scale effectively. For some models, internally funded growth is possible and ideal, but for others, access to outside capital is essential.

For example, expanding into new states might require significant upfront investment. You could take 20 years to grow organically, but with the right capital, you could do it in three. The faster path keeps your top talent engaged and excited, whereas slower growth risks losing your best people to more dynamic opportunities.

Rate how your organization is managing growth capital:

1: This is a major constraint holding back our growth.	2: We have access to some capital, but it's not sufficient or well-leveraged.	3: We're in great shape here.

15. Relationships

Elevating relationships requires psychological safety and a willingness to take risks. In a healthy organization, employees feel safe to speak their minds, share their perspectives, and advocate for what's best for the company—even if it involves difficult truths.

The key is aligning your head and heart with the organization's greater good—not being abrasive or pursuing self-serving agendas. If someone can't embrace that alignment, they're better off finding a new organization. For everyone else, this culture of trust and transparency transforms work into something fun and fulfilling.

How elevated are your team relationships?

1: Trust and psychological safety are significant opportunities for improvement. A lot of our people operate from a place of fear or scarcity.	**2**: Things are okay, but there's room to grow. Some of our people continue to operate from a place of fear or scarcity.	**3**: Our team thrives on transparency, trust, and collaboration.

Action Plan

Here's how to move forward. Take the next 10 minutes to huddle with your team and compare answers across all the categories discussed. Tabulate your scores, and identify the **three areas that received the lowest scores**—these represent your biggest opportunities for unlocking dormant, pent-up potential.

Next, prioritize these three areas:

1. Focus on the biggest issue in the next 90 days.
2. Tackle the second-lowest scoring area in the following quarter.
3. Address the third one within nine months.

By reducing friction and removing key obstacles, you can significantly improve your organization's performance.

The goal of this exercise is to leave your team feeling energized, with a clear and actionable plan for progress.

Bloom Growth OS
GLOSSARY of Terms

90-Minute Discovery Meeting — The first step of the Bloom Growth Journey to bring together the Entrepreneur and the smallest version of the Leadership Team with a Bloom Growth Coach to determine if the Bloom Growth Operating System (BGOS) is the right fit for their business.

BGOS — Bloom Growth Operating System. An execution, communication, and relationship system for companies either growing so fast the wheels are coming off or are not growing as fast as they would like.

Bloom Growth Coach — A successful entrepreneur who works with a Leadership Team and leads them on the Bloom Growth Journey.

Bloom Growth Journey — The Bloom Growth OS path.

Bloom Integrator — Leads, manages, and helps the Leadership Team win, owns the execution of the Growth Plan, grows the business and achieves all numbers-based goals, owns the P&L, and harmoniously coordinates all systems, energy, and people.

Bloom Talk — A presentation to be shared with forums, peer groups, or business networking groups to create possibilities for business owners and their teams to address pain points that every business experiences.

Bloom Weekly — 90-minute "Win the Week" meeting occurring weekly with focused tactical execution.

Check-In Questionnaire — Pre-work for team members to fill out prior to BGOS planning sessions to share expectations and outcomes, celebrate wins, and build the O&O List.

LMW — *Lead, manage,* and help direct reports *win.*

O&Os — Opportunities and Obstacles. Items for immediate discussion during the Bloom Weekly go on the short-term list, while O&Os to be addressed later in the quarter are placed on the long-term list (also called the "parking lot").

QPs — Quarterly Priorities (goals).

RPRS — Right people, right seats.

Visionary — Typically the business owner and/or founder of the company who understands the industry, inspires culture, shapes core values, grows strategic relationships, and spots future trends.

Bloom Weekly

- **Check-In** — Opening for Bloom Weekly meetings. Team members share their most meaningful personal and professional best and their feelings about it from the last 7 days. 5 *minutes.*
- **KPIs** — Key Performance Indicators. Weekly activities that allow the Leadership Team visibility in the

regular running and growing of the business to produce and predict the quarterly and annual growth
goals. 5 *minutes.*

- **Quarterly Priorities** — Most important special proj-
ects/goals for building a better business. Tracked
weekly to achieve in 90 days. 5 *minutes.*
- **Headlines** — Sharing of company news about customers, employees, and/or vendors. 5 *minutes.*
- **To-Dos** — Action items based on the most sacred
promises made to each other as a team, completed
on a weekly basis. 5 *minutes.*
- **O&O List** — List of opportunities and obstacles. Used
to compile both short-term and long-term O&Os so
that the team can leverage opportunities and remove obstacles together each week to 3D (Discover,
Discuss, and Decide). 60 *minutes.*
- **3D** — Discover, Discuss, Decide. The best practice
for *discovering* the root cause, *discussing* the desired
outcome, and making a permanent and inspiring *decision.* Decisions are captured as actionable to-dos
that are due at the next Bloom Weekly.
- **Wrap-Up** — Review the list of to-dos and what needs
to be communicated to other teams. Ask how the
meeting could improve and add those items to the
check-in for the following Bloom Weekly. 5 *minutes.*

Bloom Growth OS 8 Essentials

The Bloom Growth 8 Essentials — The eight key areas
that every business needs to focus on. These are:

- Growth Plan
- People
- Sales & Marketing

- Meetings
- Finance & Data
- Process
- Technology
- Relationships

1. Growth Plan — A company's blueprint for growing and how to get there. Includes the What, How, Why, 5-Year Vision, 3-Year Future, 1-Year Plan, and 90-Day Plan:

- **What** — The simplest, humble, gritty, raw, authentic way to say what the organization does.
- **How** — The simplest 3–7 words about how you do what you do.
- **Why** — Heartfelt statement that describes why the organization does what it does beyond making money.
- **5-Year Vision** — The north star for growing the company that is both qualitative (meaningful from the heart) and quantitative (something you can measure).
- **3-Year Future** — Creates a picture of what it will look like in the future through numbers-based growth goals and future possibilities and is used for recruiting, onboarding and retaining top talent.
- **1-Year Plan** — The numbers-based growth goals and the 4–7 most important Annual Goals for the entire organization to accomplish by the end of your year.
- **90-Day Plan** — The quarterly numbers-based growth goals and 4–7 Quarterly Priorities, which are the most important special projects for the entire organization to accomplish in the next quarter.

2. People — People are the foundation of your business. Without people, you don't have a business. Your business is made up of your clients, the vendors you work with, and most especially your employees.

- **Core Values** — Characteristics of humans that have always been true of your organization and used as relationship filters for customers, employees, and vendors.
- **Ideal Team Structure** — Organization chart to scale the business over the next 12 months with seats, roles and responsibilities for each team member.
- **Management Training** — Communication strategy for servant leaders to help their direct reports win.
- **Reviews, Raises, & Incentives** — Strategy for team member retention and development.

3. Sales and Marketing — Tools for going after new clients, and an equal amount of emphasis for retaining and growing existing clients and customers.

- **Sales Referral Strategy** — For determining who can give your company referrals, what differentiates your company, how to train and role play the ask, the best way to make the request, and the timing—so you can forecast and budget for growth.
- **Ideal Client** — The target audience we like and want to do business with such that a go-to-market strategy is developed and implemented.

4. Meetings — From Bloom Day 1, your meetings will transform productivity and streamline communication and execution.

- **Bloom Weekly (BW)** — A 90-minute team meeting occurring weekly with focused tactical execution.
- **Bloom Day 1** — The first full-day offsite with your Bloom Growth Coach to create the Future Ideal

Leadership Structure, 5-Year Vision, Deeper Bond & Connection as a team, alignment on the most important priorities for the quarter, and launching the Bloom Weekly meeting.

- **Bloom Day 30** — The second full-day offsite with your Bloom Growth Coach. Team shares letters from their future selves; get introduced to "Stories We Tell Ourselves"; identify weekly KPIs to track progress toward 3-Year, 1-Year, and 90-Day Growth Goals, and draft their initial What, How, and Why.

- **Bloom Day 60** — The third full-day offsite with your Bloom Growth Coach where the team gets introduced to Relationship Traps, Personal Energy Audit, Core Values, 3-Year Future, and Annual Goals.

- **Bloom Day 90** — The fourth full-day offsite with your Bloom Growth Coach to review and learn from the previous quarter, set new Quarterly Priorities, learn how to share Bloom Growth OS to the whole team, finalize the Growth Plan, and sign the north star document.

- **Bloom Quarterly** — An all-day offsite leadership team planning session with your Bloom Growth Coach focused on building a better business, setting new Quarterly Priorities, elevating relationships, and strengthening team performance such that your results and relationships are improving every quarter.

- **Bloom Annual** — A two-day offsite where the leadership team gathers with their Bloom Growth Coach to create alignment, clarity, and a clear plan of action for the quarter and year ahead. This annual kickoff session emphasizes relationship growth and the compounding power of prioritization.

- **Departmental Bloom Quarterly** — A three- to four-hour department planning session focused on priorities, KPIs, process, and people. The goal is to improve the department and build better relationships within the team.
- **1:1 Meetings** — Any recurring meetings between two people.
- **Sales Bloom Weekly** — Departmental Bloom Weekly meeting specific to the Sales Team that focuses primarily on KPIs.
- **Engineering Bloom Weekly** — Departmental Bloom Weekly specific to the Engineering Team that works with the existing development process (often a version of agile).
- **Quarterly Alignment** — One-on-one coaching between every manager and direct report with the outcome of connectedness, review of Quarterly Priorities, Roles & Responsibilities, To-Dos, KPIs, and Core Values.
- **Monthly P&L and Cash Flow** — Agenda for the leadership team to be in-the-know and proactive with the company's finances.
- **All Org Gathering** — An hour-long meeting once per quarter where you get on the same page as an organization.

5. **Finance & Data** — Tools for getting the right data at the right time, which allows you to make proactive decisions.

- **Growth Goals** — The top 3 to 5 numbers-based outcomes or results for your business. Targets are set for 3-Year, 1-Year, and every Quarter.
- **KPIs** — Weekly key performance indicators for the regular growing and running of the business.

Measuring the activities that need to happen every week in order to achieve your quarterly and annual growth goals.

- **Cash Optimization** — Learn how to read the profit & loss statement, balance sheet, and cash flow statement, and understand how leadership decisions influence and shift these seven key financial levers: volume, price, COGS, expenses, A/R, inventory and A/P.
- **Financial Plan** — A forecast that outlines expected revenue and a budget that guides planned spending.

6. Process — Improve the speed and quality of easily accessed recurring processes, such that they are regularly updated, securely stored, supported by version control, and have established permission settings.

7. Technology — Optimizing your tech stack internally to eliminate overlapping subscriptions and leveraging externally to make the client and customer experience seamless.

8. Relationships — By embracing and cultivating Bloom's modern Relationship Curriculum, which focuses on human flourishing, leaders become more emotionally intelligent individuals. Teams become more connected and aligned, and the entire organization experiences deeper levels of joy and fulfillment.

Acknowledgments

To **Clay Upton** and **Jay Wilkinson**, my partners in Bloom Growth and whose invaluable insights helped shape this manuscript: You've entertained a multitude of unreasonable requests from me (Todd) over the past two to three years and have been incredibly supportive throughout. I'm deeply grateful for your generosity, positivity, and kindness. Perhaps it's no coincidence that you're both from Lincoln, Nebraska, which is most certainly the center of kindness in America. Your contributions have made this book immeasurably better.

Sheila Dodd, you are the connective tissue of our team and master wrangler of all the moving parts and people. You're so much more than a project manager—you're the glue that holds us together, harmoniously coordinating everything with your remarkable ability to see the details in the vision. I (Todd) want to personally thank you for your support as my family and I lived our three-year adventure. You keep us on track with unwavering dedication and relentless positive energy. Without you, this book would still be a great idea stuck inside the heads of a couple of visionary entrepreneurs. For you, we are profoundly thankful.

Lori Lynn, finding you as our writer and book architect was one of those perfect alignment moments. You've been so much more than a scribe this past year—you've been a true entrepreneurial partner who not only co-wrote this book but also edited it, somehow integrating ideas and input from multiple voices. Flying blind with multiple copilots toward a moving target, you managed to land the plane with remarkable skill. Without you, this book would have been super dry and boring, but you took our scattered ideas and shaped them into something we're genuinely proud of—something even we were willing to read over and over again. You were—and are—the absolute right person to capture both the practical elements and the heart of what makes Bloom Growth special.

About the Authors

TODD SMART

Co-creator of the Bloom Growth Operating System (BGOS), Todd Smart brings over 30 years of entrepreneurial experience to his work as a Growth Coach. An Entrepreneurs' Organization (EO) member since the 90s, he has built multiple successful businesses while personally guiding more than 100 leadership teams through growth transformation.

One of the architects of BGOS and the visionary for the Bloom Coaching Community, Todd is also one of the first 20 EOS Implementers®, co-founding Traction Tools (the first software solution for EOS®). With two decades as a Forum Facilitator and Trainer for EO and Young Presidents' Organization (YPO), he has learned both what works and what's missing in traditional business systems and relationships.

Todd recently completed a three-year adventure with his wife and four children, spending 18 months RVing across

North America and 18 months sailing the Caribbean—living proof that with the right people and process in place, you can build a thriving business while simultaneously having the adventure of a lifetime.

ISAIAH NOLTE

For the past decade, Isaiah Nolte has served on the Bloom Growth leadership team, working with thousands of companies across multiple industries within Bloom Growth Software to unlock their growth potential. A member of YPO (Young Presidents' Organization), he is a Bloom Growth Coach, co-creator of the Bloom Growth OS, and the leader of the Bloom Growth Coach Community.

Growing up in an entrepreneurial household in northern Minnesota, business conversations around the dinner table sparked his passion for building companies. At just 18, he founded and grew his first business.

Later, he served as a volunteer for two years with Latin American Child Care and Convoy of Hope, where he learned to speak Spanish fluently. As he helped to build schools in remote areas and assist with massive food distribution, Isaiah fell in love with the people and the country of Nicaragua. That is where he currently resides with his wife and their five children.